THE
GNOSTIC EMPIRE
STRIKES BACK

THE
GNOSTIC EMPIRE
STRIKES BACK

AN OLD HERESY FOR THE NEW AGE

PETER JONES

PUBLISHING

P.O. BOX 817 • PHILLIPSBURG • NEW JERSEY 08865-0817

Library of Congress Cataloging-in-Publication Data

Jones, Peter, 1940–
    The gnostic empire strikes back : an old heresy for the New Age / Peter Jones.
        p.   cm.
    Includes bibliographical references.
    ISBN 0-87552-285-8 (pbk.)
    1. New Age movement—Controversial literature. 2. Gnosticism—Controversial literature. 3. Christianity and other religions. 4. United States—Moral conditions. I. Title.
BP605.N48J67 1992
239'.9—dc20   92-29525

Contents

Preface   ix

1. Getting a Handle on the New Age   1

2. The Gnostic Empire Strikes Back   11

3. All You Really Need to Know
   About Ancient Gnosticism   19

4. The New Age—The Return of
   Ancient Gnosticism   43

5. Perspectives for the Planet
   and for the Church   81

"Those who cannot remember the past
are condemned to repeat it."

—George Santayana
in *The Life of Reason,*
Volume 2: Reason and Society

"As well as I can . . . I will briefly and clearly
describe the position of the present false teachers.
. . . I am neither practiced in writing nor trained
in rhetoric, but my love for you and yours encour-
ages me to bear my witness about these teachings
which have been hidden till the present, but have
now by the grace of God come to light."

—Irenaeus,
missionary, church-planter in the South of France,
Bishop of Lyons, 130-200,
in *Against Heresies,* Preface 2-3

Preface

Have you ever asked yourself any of the following questions?

Why is homosexuality on the rise? Why is it endorsed by *Time Magazine,* promoted on publicly funded radio, and featured in children's comic strips—with great moral fervor and in the name of democracy? Why is feminism such a powerful force today? Why is this movement developing its own goddess spirituality? Why is witchcraft taught in certain Californian school districts? Why is feminist spirituality making enormous inroads into Christianity? Why is abortion a vitally important part of the feminist manifesto? Is ecology just a neutral concern about the survival of the planet, or does it too have a religious agenda? Why is American Indian nature religion being actively promoted? Why is the work ethic no longer working? Why is multiculturalism and political correctness so important on many college campuses? Are these seemingly disconnected issues related in any way to the so-called

New Age Movement? Why are the numerous New Age spiritual techniques for healing, peace of mind, and self-knowledge being publicized so vigorously in the media, and more and more utilized in the business world and the armed forces?

The real question is this: Are these apparently disconnected issues really part of a coherent pagan ideology poised to impose its religious belief system on the New World Order (the Age of Aquarius) of the twenty-first century? The following comparison of New Age objectives with the pagan Gnosticism that dominated society in the first three centuries of the Christian church would answer yes to that most important question.

This study's aim is thus:

- to *clarify* the true nature of the forces opposing Christians today and to demonstrate their interconnectedness;
- to *warn* the church of the battle that lies ahead in order that Christians might be prepared;
- to *encourage* believers to "fight the good fight" using the weapons of faith, particularly the sword of God's Word, by which pagan Gnosticism was once already put to flight from the early church, and by which it will be put to flight again.

1

Getting a Handle on the New Age

BEATLEMANIA

I was raised in Liverpool, England, during the fifties. One of my first friends at Quarry Bank High School was named John. For six years we shared the same kind of humor, wrote the same kind of idiotic poetry, fooled around a lot, and played music together. Banal information, I suppose—except that my friend's last name was Lennon.

I beat the Beatles to America by two months, but their arrival made a much bigger splash than mine. To my European eyes, America in 1964 was a very religious Christian country. People used churches instead of pubs as landmarks when they gave directions. Public prayer and the use of God's name were commonplace. But during the sixties and early seventies, as my friend John wrote and sang of LSD, Hinduism, and global love in unforgettable hits such as "Lucy in the Sky with Diamonds," I witnessed firsthand a mixed bag of liberation movements: of blacks, of drugs, of sex, of women, and of religion.

According to many who travel, southern France is the nicest place on the face of the earth. During the seventies and eighties I lived, taught, and raised a family in the south of France. But everything has a down side. Urbane, humanistic, secular France was not the easiest of places for Christian witness. We were soon made to understand that it was indecorous to mention one's faith in polite society. In 1988 the American tennis player Michael Chang, then seventeen, won Roland Garros, the French hard court championships. Over the public address system, and on live national TV, he thanked his coach, his mom and dad, and most of all "the Lord Jesus Christ, without whom," he said, "I am nothing." The seventeen thousand fans booed and whistled. The official TV news that night highlighted Chang's short testimony by setting it mockingly against a musical background of Handel's "Hallelujah Chorus."

In the eighties, in Europe, the four spiritual laws of atheistic humanism disintegrated: existentialism, Freudianism, evolutionism, and Marxism. In their wake lies a huge spiritual vacuum.

When my family and I returned to the United States in 1991, we discovered that America was just as religious, but a lot less Christian! Out of the seeds of the liberation movements of the sixties had sprouted a new religion, which calls itself the "New Age." A deranged fundamentalist shot John Lennon, but the yellow submarine is surfacing through the murky waters of changing morals, warmed by the light of the inner being. It would be a monumental error to think that the New Age is just another passing fad of West Coast spiritual exotica. It will not go away. It will no doubt be the spirituality that will fill the void of godless Europe, and perhaps the whole world. For while America still exercises the dominant role of international leadership, its Christian moral leadership has virtually disappeared, displaced by a leadership that is immoral and anti-Christian. Americans, so keen on discovering their roots, have nevertheless cut themselves off from their Christian roots. The resulting fruit is withered and rotten. America is still number one, but unfortunately she is number one in homosexuality, feminism, divorce, the destruction of family values, abortion, political correctness, and the occult humanistic spirituality of New Age religion. With leadership like this, the New Age is most likely to become *the* dominant global religion of the twenty-first century. It would now seem that my friend John was quite a New Age prophet. The hit-song "Imagine" says it all. There Lennon asks us to imagine:

> no heaven . . .
> no hell . . .
> no countries . . .
> no possessions . . .

no greed . . .
no hunger . . .
no religion.[1]

In this new Age of Aquarius, where there is neither good nor evil, the ultimate liberation of mankind will finally be realized—liberation from ethics, from guilt, from sexual norms, and from God. Only one religious option will *not* be allowed to live life in peace, namely, biblical Christianity.

Christians too should begin to imagine—imagine realistically what this one world could look like without the preserving effect of a strong Christian church. Based on the church's past experience with Gnosticism, Christians can take stock of the threat posed by the New Age. To be forewarned is to be forearmed.

How Do You Catch A Slippery Eel?

The tolerant, soft-sell promotion of freedom, equality, spirituality, responsible ecology, and international peace gives the impression that the New Age is not an organized religion. It prides itself on its myriad groups and multiple techniques. Such a slippery customer is hard to pin down. By its vast variety and by not calling itself a religion or a church the New Age has spread unchecked, cleverly avoiding the restraints of church-state separation placed on Christianity. Its only concern is "human spirituality." Thus the public library in our town has New Age newspapers in its free literature bin, whereas specifically "religious" Christian newspapers go directly to the garbage can. A dazzling diversity—go into any New Age bookshop—tends to mask any underlying unity, and the extent of its agenda in its relationship with other social movements is not always obvious. But as time goes on, and the movement flexes its muscles in public, there are signs of deep tentacular power and ideological coherence.

Without the distance of some historical perspective, understanding the true nature, the real intentions, the coherent agenda, and the vast scope of a largely secretive and world-wide religious network would not be possible. Many excellent books document and describe New Age phenomena. This book seeks to analyze the scope and ideological coherence of the movement not from pure description or prophetic speculation, but from the vantage point of real history.

Historical study can seem daunting. There are other more pressing things to do. But before you put this book down, remember that a careful look at the past may be the only way to gain a clear understanding of the present, not to mention, the future—before, of course, it is too late! Let me invite you, then, to step back just for a moment. The effort, I believe, will prove well worth it, for the findings are mind-boggling.

An Old Heresy for the New Age

In ancient Gnosticism we can observe both bewildering diversity and, with the advantage of hindsight, a consistent heretical agenda. When the Christian gospel moved beyond Judaism, it came face to face with another religious world, that of Greco-Roman paganism. Back then there were few (if any) atheists; everyone was a believer in some form of deity.[2] The confrontation between religious beliefs was total, the shock often violent. Pagans either rejected the gospel out of hand, which often led to the persecution and physical elimination of Christians, or forsook their pagan gods, burned their magical books and amulets on the spot, and adopted the Christian faith. In the second and third centuries A.D., however, Christianity became more and more the dominant religion, and the pressures of the pagan world made themselves felt in subtler ways. Certain "Christian" teachers sought to accommodate the faith to this pagan religion, in spite of the apostle Paul's warning to the converted pagans in Corinth: "What harmony is there between Christ and Belial . . . between the temple of God and idols?" (2 Cor. 6:15-16); "[between] the Lord's table and the table of demons[?]" (1 Cor. 10:21). The resulting perversion, "Christian Gnosticism," made great strides throughout the Western world until it was exposed by the untiring work of certain church fathers as a pernicious and diabolical heresy. With the 20/20 vision of hindsight, the analysis of ancient Gnosticism, both in its pagan and Christian forms, gives us a complete picture of the underlying coherence of its humanistic world-and-life view. When that is set alongside New Age beliefs, the results are alarming. We are suddenly confronted with

6

a many-headed monster intent on obliterating Christian faith.

LIFE AND DEATH CONSEQUENCES

The following pages lay out evidence that the New Age is in fact a modern form of ancient Gnosticism. If that is the case, there are a number of questions that concern you directly: What if the New Age is not new at all? What if, having swept the world clean of one demon (atheistic Marxism), the church falls prey to seven more? What if the New Age is actually a more potent form of ancient pagan Gnosticism, whose Satanic dimensions and spiritual bankruptcy led so many astray in the past before it was exposed and denounced by the early church?

If the New Age is a reinvigorated version of paganism, one of whose goals is to infiltrate the church, then every Christian should be alerted, for its effects would likely be disastrous. Consider the following probable consequences:

- Our world is entering a new period of spiritual, demonic delusion cavorting about in the fake clothes of spiritual renewal.
- In step with a general optimism about the New World Order of the third millennium, such spiritual delusion could quickly sweep the globe, dragging millions into spiritual death.

- A serious infiltration of error into the Christian church may threaten unsuspecting believers, including our own children, with theological confusion and spiritual defeat.
- Difficult days may lie ahead for Christians who refuse to compromise. Perhaps, rather than the great advances of the Christian faith by the year 2000 touted by many mission strategists and statesmen, Christians one day, maybe sooner than later, would be considered a bothersome and dangerous minority group threatening the peace of universal tolerance for all kinds of faiths and lifestyles. Even New Age tolerance has its limits! I am not a prophet, and I dearly hope I am wrong. But the phenomenal growth of this movement and the explicit menacing threats of New Age leaders against traditional "intractable" Christianity,[3] form an equation whose stubborn logic is difficult to avoid. This equation leads me to believe that those who profess absolute truth, the specific Creator and Redeemer God of the Bible, and biblical ethical behavior will be silenced by any means, in accord with the expedient norms of new-look Aquarian ethics.
- Christians should understand what is taking place now, both to avoid these chilling consequences, if that is still possible, and to recognize the level of commitment and public testimony required should these grim days come upon us.

8

- Those Christians who stand firm will be driven back to a fresh understanding of "the faith once delivered to the saints," especially since that faith was articulated in a pagan world very much like the one that ours is rapidly becoming. A renewed and realistic awareness of "the mystery of iniquity" would not bring defeatism. On the contrary, it would promote an even greater conviction of the truth, and thus of the final victory of Jesus Christ who looked directly into the eyes of evil and was victorious.

Such a fresh understanding of the faith cannot be developed in the confines of this short book.[4] Its purpose is more modest. The immediate pressing need is to awaken Christian believers to the true face of the enemy. Too many are asleep. Too many are immobilized by the thought that, like the economy, everything is bound to get better. Too many have confused the American dream of financial ease with the goals of the kingdom of God. Besides, looking at the mystery of evil is hardly enjoyable. Indeed it is downright oppressive, like having to watch violent, pornographic movies in order to develop guidelines for Christian family TV use. No one enjoys negative criticism. It is much easier to deal with positive issues. But look at the times in which we live. Most readers of this book will be called upon to witness to their faith in the so-called Age of Aquarius. The understanding of error is therefore an imperious necessity. However, one of the unexpected blessings that comes from the struggle with heresy is a clearer grasp of the truth. When the church has had the courage to stand against heresy, it has always emerged stronger in its faithfulness to its Lord. May this encounter with error create a renewed love and devotion to Christ in whom are hidden all the treasures of wisdom and *gnosis* (knowledge).

NOTES

1. Tal Brooke, "The Emerging Reality of a New World Order," *S.C.P. Journal* 16, 2 (1991): 15, notes that the United Nations funded the playing of this song simultaneously on thousands of radio stations throughout the world on the anniversary of Lennon's death.

2. No doubt in the third millennium, as in the days of ancient paganism, everyone will also be a "believer." The confrontation will be between the gods. Interestingly, the early twentieth-century French author and philosopher Andre Malraux, in the midst of generalized European atheism and secularism, prophesied that the twenty-first century would be a century of religious commitment.

3. See Texe Marrs, *Dark Secrets of the New Age* (Westchester, Ill.: Crossway, 1987), 136-51, and the pioneering work of Constance Cumbey, *The Hidden Dangers of the Rainbow: The New Age Movement and Our Coming Age of Barbarism* (Lafayette, La.: Huntington House, 1983), 50, 56, 113, 143.

4. I intend to develop a major study of Gnosticism and the New Age in the not-too-distant future, as well as a book on the New Testament's answers to Gnostic and New Age thought.

2

The Gnostic Empire Strikes Back

Paganism is on the rise. Inconceivably, it threatens to become a flood tide in Christendom, even in "Christian" America. In our day the pagan Gnostic empire is striking back. What incredible irony! Whereas the old, once-pagan, godless Roman Empire became Christian, America, founded on God-honoring principles by orthodox Protestant Christians, is moving with alarming speed to embrace the very paganism that ancient Rome discarded. *Christendom* (that general acceptance of the norms and structures associated with the Christian faith that has characterized the Western world for fifteen hundred years) is *on the wane.*[1] A new (though it turns out to be not-so-new) religion, the New Age, for a New World Order, is *on the rise.* Its sparkling promise of newness virtually guarantees its success in a civilization jaded by hot and cold wars, by contemporary worldwide economic recession, and by the seemingly intractable problems of poverty and ecology. Old-style materialism

11

(Marxism) is in total disarray. Capitalism appears helpless before Third World hunger, Western urban chaos, and the threat of worldwide ecological disaster. Materialism in all its forms has created spiritual hunger. The house is being swept clean. People are looking for new answers, new laws, and new faces in politics. So why not try a new religion?

THE END OF CHRISTENDOM?

What would *you* like on *your* tombstone? Try "Vicisti Galilaee"—"You have conquered, Galilean." This phrase is surely high on the all-time list of "famous last words." It is attributed to the dying Emperor Flavius Claudius Julianus (A.D. 364), affectionately known to his enemies as Julian the Apostate. Ever since his death the world has been under the impression that Julian's last-gasp admission of defeat before the conquering Jesus signaled the once-for-all demise of paganism.[2]

But now the world is in for a surprise!

To be sure, paganism had seen its day. Julian's uncle, Constantine the Great, as Roman emperor from 312 to 337, had recognized the amazing victory of Christianity by proclaiming it the official religion of the empire. From ignominious beginnings in a feeding trough somewhere in the far-flung Roman province of Judea, the Christian faith, had turned the ancient world upside-down. In three hundred years, against all expectations, Christianity had become the official religion of pagan, imperial

Rome. When he became emperor in 361, Julian, the last committed pagan ruler of Rome, tried for three years to turn the ancient world right side up again—to no avail. The original spiritual power of the Christian faith, and the unstinting efforts of Christian thinkers such as Irenaeus, Hippolytus, Tertullian, Marcellus, and Athanasius, who fought tooth and nail against the infiltration of pagan Gnosticism into the church, meant that nothing could stop the church's march through the Western world. For the record, Julian's successor, Valentinian I, was an orthodox, "Athanasian" Christian, and although paganism would continue in the empire, Christendom was on the move.

In 1980 there were 1.4 billion Christians in the world, and serious estimates put that figure at 2 billion by the year 2000.[3] Indeed, it has seemed for one and a half millennia that with Julian's passing, the paganism he dearly loved had also forever passed away—until, oddly, the last quarter of the twentieth century!

Today Tom Williams, priest of the Church of All Worlds, labels Christendom the "Christian interlude."[4] Williams is surely suffering from delirium. Nothing can stop the growth of Christianity as we move with new missions strategies into the third millennium. But the New Age people are deadly serious. This Christian interlude, called in astrological circles "the Age of Pisces" (the Fish, the historic symbol of the Christian faith), fueled by masculine, *yang* energy, is now at an end. It is being superseded by the feminine *yin* energy of the Age of Aquarius.[5]

13

That is the underlying message of Michael Wood's Public Television series, *"Legacy,"* according to which Christianity never quite succeeded in crushing the pagan nature religions, which now come back to offer us genuine ecological, spiritual, and planetary salvation. From his Christian perspective, another well-known English journalist, Malcolm Muggeridge, also recognized the death of Christendom: "We are living through the last days of Christendom. It's like the last days of Rome. And as the west comes to an end, the reasons for its coming to an end will become apparent."[6] Those reasons, I believe, have now become apparent! That pagan "Gnostic" empire, personified by Julian and so roundly defeated by the early church many centuries ago, is now openly and brazenly striking back. Shirley MacLaine, televangelist for the New Age, in her best seller *Going Within* (1989) states that there is nothing new about the New Age. This is why she can go on to say, "[Ancient] Christian Gnostics operated with New Age knowledge."[7]

EAST MEETS WEST: A POTENT BREW

"Mythology is making a comeback"—not the modern kind, such as, "There's a giant alligator living in the sewers of Manhattan," but the ancient mythology of Egypt, Greece, and Rome. Such is the considered judgment of columnist Deanne Stillman.[8] Professor Giovanni Filoramo, a noted authority on ancient Gnosticism, states that in our contemporary culture we are witnessing "a rediscovery of Gnosis."[9] The highly regarded German specialist Hans Jonas, in his definitive work, *The Gnostic Religion* (1958), describes the formation of Gnosticism in the centuries just before the birth of Christ as the meeting of the mysticism of ancient Eastern religions with the rational culture of the Greek West.

> What we do witness at the period roughly corresponding with the beginnings of Christianity is an explosion of the East. Like long-pent-up waters its force broke through the Hellenistic crust and flooded the ancient world, flowing into the established Greek forms and filling them with their content, besides creating their own new beds. The metamorphosis of Hellenism into a religious oriental culture was set on foot.[10]

As far as I can tell, Shirley MacLaine has not read Jonas. But her observation makes me think that we are reliving today the same kind of conditions as those prevailing at the time of the early church. "In my opinion," she observes, "this New Age is the time when the intuitive beliefs of the East and the scientific thinking of the West could meet and join— the twain wed at last. For me, both are necessary, and both are desirable."[11] In the same way, Tal Brooke, a proto-New-Ager of the sixties, now a converted Christian, describes his mystical experiences through LSD and Indian Hinduism as a composite of the best of the East blended with the most radical breakthroughs in the West—the new physics, new forms of psychology, and all sorts of spiritual

15

technology.[12] The new spirituality of the West is, according to Theodore Roszak, a New Age spokesman, "the greatest adventure of our age" and "the reclamation and renewal of the old Gnosis."[13]

Other writers have been even more explicit about the return of Gnosticism. In the words of one observer, "Gnosticism is experiencing something of a revival, despite its historical status within Christianity as a vanquished Christian heresy."[14] James Robinson, noted New Testament scholar and Director of the Institute for Antiquity and Christianity, speaks of Gnosticism as an apparently inaccessible religion of late antiquity, which nevertheless "continues to emerge in new garb and unexpected ways in the midst of our technological world today."[15]

Are these suggestions true? Is the New Age a revival of ancient Gnosticism? Is there any substance to these claims? Because these statements have not been followed by any significant documentation, we need to examine the Gnostic system itself. This, I hasten to add, will not be an abstract study of an ancient religious system for purely historical interest. Our aim is to gain a more complete understanding of the scope and coherence of Gnosticism in its current manifestation, the so-called New Age.

NOTES

1. In 1986 Malcolm Muggeridge declared, "Christendom is over, but not Christ." In "Dialogues with Malcolm Muggeridge," *S.C.P. Journal* 16, 2 (1991):35.

2. Even as late as 1967, a commendation from *The New Yorker* magazine on the back cover of Hans Jonas's milestone study, *The Gnostic Religion* (Boston: Beacon Press, 1958) does not recognize the Gnostic revival in the New Age Movement: "A fascinating exposition, with copious quotations, of what is known as Gnosticism. . . . Dr. Jonas writes with authority, passion and precision about *this long-forgotten religion*" (emphasis mine).

3. According to the highly regarded *World Christian Encyclopedia,* ed. D. B. Barrett (Oxford and New York: Oxford University Press, 1982), 4. That is still, however, only 32.8 percent of the world's population.

4. Cited in Dave Bass, "Drawing Down the Moon," *Christianity Today,* April 1991, 17.

5. Shirley MacLaine, *Going Within: A Guide for Inner Transformation* (New York: Bantam Books, 1989), 189.

6. "Dialogues with Malcolm Muggeridge," 39.

7. *Going Within,* 29-30.

8. Deanne Stillman, "The Many Masks of Camille Paglia," *Los Angeles Times Magazine,* February 16, 1992, 28.

9. Giovanni Filoramo, *A History of Gnosticism,* trans. A. Alcock (London: Basil Blackwell, 1990), xiii. Of the almost seven thousand titles in David M. Scholer, *Nag Hammadi Bibliography 1948-1968* (Leiden: Brill, 1971—see also the many supplements in *Novum Testamentum*), only one title—the short but incisive article by E. and P. Hinlicky, "Gnosticism: Old and New" *Dialog* 28, 1 (1989): 12-17—suggests the thesis I am proposing in this book.

10. H. Jonas, *The Gnostic Religion* (Boston: Beacon Press, 1963), 23.

11. MacLaine, *Going Within,* 99.

12. Tal Brooke, *When the World Will Be as One* (Eugene, Oreg.: Harvest House, 1989), 48.

13. T. Roszak, *Where the Wasteland Ends: Politics and Transcendence in Post-Industrial Society* (New York: Doubleday, 1972), 262.

14. Douglas R. Groothuis, *Revealing the New Age Jesus*

(Downers Grove, Ill.: InterVarsity, 1990), 75.

15. See the cover of Kurt Rudolph, *Gnosis: The Nature and History of an Ancient Religion* (Edinburgh: T. and T. Clark, 1983).

3

All You Really Need to Know About Ancient Gnosticism

BEWILDERING DIVERSITY

There are no supermarkets in today's Russia. Shoppers have at most only two choices—take it or leave it! You grab the one brand of cheese on the shelf (if there is any), or you go without cheese for a few weeks. In the West, in addition to the omnipresent supermarkets for everything, from food (fifty kinds of breakfast cereal)[1] and drugs (twelve different kinds of antacid relief—one for every 4.17 kinds of cereal!) to automotive parts, the New Age brings you supermarketing for the mind. Pick up any New Age local advertiser. The list is mind-boggling: soul memory kinesiology; life enrichment; contact with extraterrestrial multidimensional masters; a doctor of divinity degree from the Religious Science Center; shamanic awakening; astrological counseling; channeling by Narena; nonhypnotic past-life regression; hypnotic past-life regression; breast enlargement by visualization; Jin Shin Jyutsu; deep tissue, meditative, polarity and reflexology massage. And the list goes on.[2] How could anyone hope to understand the New Age?

Take heart. It was just the same with Gnosticism. There is nothing new under the sun, including the New Age. In ancient Athens, instead of bookstores and "centers" the discriminating "very religious" shopper was offered altars, all with their own "mysteries," spiritual techniques, promises of better life from priest or priestess gurus in the "knowsis." One can almost hear the apostle Paul chuckle with disbelief as he wanders around this ancient Athenian spiritual supermarket and congratulates the locals on their multifarious religiosity.[3] Paul's experience was not unique. While the early church fathers found proof of the Gnostics' fraudulent theology in their manifold contradictory systems and opposing doctrines, the Gnostics congratulated themselves on the great richness of their diversity and their tolerance of many approaches to truth.[4]

A PROFOUND COHERENCE

Like the bewildering diversity of present New Age religion, ancient Gnosticism was a kaleidoscopic mixture of many varied traditions. However, Kurt Rudolph, professor of history of religions at Karl Marx University, Leipzig, in his authoritative work, *Gnosis*,[5] identifies within the perplexing diversity what he calls the "central myth." The forty-seven recently discovered (1948) Gnostic documents from the region of Nag Hammadi, Egypt, give a firsthand witness both to this central myth and to the great diversity of which ancient Gnosticism is composed. What Gnosticism taught about the world, redemption, Christ, God, sexuality, and spiritual techniques provides us with a working (though by no means exhaustive) definition of the main features of this system of thought. When these features are set against those of the New Age, the parallels are most impressive.

COSMOLOGY: THE WORLD, A COSMIC GOOF

The world is in trouble. The trouble is not due to some peripheral or temporary malfunction, like a car engine with dirty spark plugs. Nor is it even the result of human moral failing, like a car with a drunken driver. The trouble lies within the very fabric of the universe. The problem is that *there is a car!* The physical universe was never meant to be. Its existence, its creation if you will, resulted from a cosmic "goof" committed by the foolish Creator God (the Demiurge) of the Bible. The ancient Gnostics understood very well that if their system was going to work, they would have to get rid of the God of the Bible. This explains the extremist anticreation and anti-Old Testament sentiment found in certain Gnostic texts. Yaldaboath (an obvious parody of Jahweh), the Chief Archon

(Ruler-Creator) is vilified and mocked with a disdain bordering on hate. According to one of the recently discovered Gnostic texts from Nag Hammadi, the so-called *Hypostasis of the Archons,* God the Creator is represented as blind, ignorant, arrogant, the source of envy and the Father of Death. His arrogance is fully demonstrated when he cries out, "It is I who am god; there is none [apart from me],"[6] a clear reference to the claims of the Lord, the Creator of the heavens and the earth, in Isaiah 45:18 (cp. 41:4; 42:8; 43:10; 44:6; 45:18). Creation is interpreted in "all the Gnostic texts as an act of unspeakable pride (hybris) on the part of the Demiurge,"[7] who will be punished at the end of the age.[8] Another example of this antisemitic, anti-Old Testament bias is found in another Nag Hammadi text, the *Apocalypse of Adam.* The Jews are the descendants of Shem, i.e., unregenerate Cainites. The Gentiles (Christian Gnostics) are descended from Seth, the true spiritual line of descent.[9] The Creator God is an impostor, masquerading as the true unknowable God. Sparks of authentic divinity were accidentally infused into humanity by the bungling Demiurge. Gnostic believers know that they are imprisoned in evil matter, and they need to find a way of escape from its cosmic structures. Historically, the Gnostics escaped by throwing off the shackles of the Old Testament and of the God of Israel. In this newfound freedom, they reinterpreted the New Testament according to the religious world view of the pagan culture around them.

22

REDEMPTION: THE GOD OF THE BIBLE WILL NOT SAVE YOU—KNOWING YOURSELF WILL

Of my five daughters, three have theological names. Anastasia ("resurrection") is firmly orthodox, but the other two, Sophia ("wisdom") and Zoe ("life") describe the female principle that represents salvation for the redeemed Gnostic! My wife and I have some explaining to do!

Just as the spirit-endowed Eve saved Adam, so final salvation will be brought through female power. According to the newly found Nag Hammadi text *Hypostasis of the Archons,* Dame Wisdom, the heavenly Eve, enters the snake called the "Instructor"[10] and teaches Adam and Eve the true way of salvation. Another Nag Hammadi text, *On the Origin of the World,* describes the serpent as "the one who is wiser than all of them."[11] This is a recurring theme in the Gnostic literature.[12] The serpent is the redeemer. The God of Scripture is the evil usurper. "But of what sort is this God?" asked the exasperated author of the *Testimony of Truth.*

> First [he] envied Adam that he should eat from the tree of knowledge. And, secondly, he said, "Adam, where are you?" And God does not have foreknowledge, that is, since he did not know this from the beginning? And afterwards he said, "Let us cast him [out] of this place lest he eat of the tree of life and live forever." Surely he has shown himself to be a malicious envier. (47.15-30)

It is further argued that when Moses lifted up the serpent in the wilderness, he was showing

23

(whether he realized it or not) that the serpent in the garden was Christ (49.5). This is redemptive history stood on its head, like a Satanist cross in a black mass. Irenaeus (A.D. 130–200), who had first-hand experience of Gnostic teaching, was no doubt correct when he called those who blaspheme the Creator "agents of Satan."[13] Hippolytus, in a graphic description of certain Gnostics who called themselves the Naasenes (from the Hebrew *nahas,* "snake"), or Ophites (from the Greek *ophis,* "snake") that is, the worshipers of the serpent, suggests that this was by no means a peripheral movement.[14]

The Kingdom of God Is Inside of You. Though caught in matter, humanity can once again become part of the universal whole by a process of self-knowledge and self-realization (which, according to Genesis, is the root of sin). This quest is based upon what Birger Pearson calls "the heart and core of the Gnostic religion,"[15]—the consubstantiality of the self with God. In this system Christ does not deal with sin by his vicarious atonement. He comes rather as a revealer of *gnosis,* the knowledge of one's own divinity. The human plight is not moral offenses against a holy God, but ignorance of human origins and human potential. According to the account of origins in the Valentinian (Gnostic) *Gospel of Truth:* "Ignorance . . . brought about anguish and terror. And the anguish grew solid like a fog, so that no one was able to see" (17.10-16). Thus the moral obedience of Jesus that led him to the cross has no

24

significance in Gnostic thought. Certainly Jesus died on the cross, but only the Gnostic knows that the real Christ actually sat on the branch of a tree, watching and laughing. The *Apocalypse of Peter* says:

> He whom you saw on the tree, glad and laughing, this is the living Jesus. But the one in whose hands and feet they drive the nails is the fleshly part which is the substitute being put to shame, the one who came into being in his likeness. . . . Be strong, for you are the one to whom these mysteries have been given, to know them through revelation that he whom they crucified is the first-born, and the home of demons, and the stony vessel [?] in which they dwell, of Elohim, of the cross which is under the Law. But he who stands near him is the living Savior.[16]

Since Christ did not die, there is no physical resurrection. As the *Testimony of Truth* 36.29-30 says, "[Do not] expect, therefore, [the] carnal resurrection, which is destruction."[17] Redemption is not the miraculous transformation of the creation. It is a new self-understanding. As Pearson remarks, "The Gnostic, though . . . divine, must also become divine by the event of saving gnosis . . . self-knowledge."[18] This is why the "living Jesus" of the *Gospel of Thomas* says to his disciples:

> If those who lead you [no doubt orthodox Christianity[19]] say to you, "See, the Kingdom is in the sky," then the birds of the air will precede you. If they say to you, "It is in the sea," then the fish will precede you. Rather the kingdom is inside of

you. . . . When you come to know yourselves, then you will become known and you will realize that it is you who are the sons of the living Father. But if you will not know yourselves, you dwell in poverty and it is you who are that poverty.[20]

Gnostic believers are "saved" when they realize who they are—a part of the divine; possessing within themselves the kingdom; capable of anything; and untrammeled by human traditions, creational structures, or divine laws. It follows that part of self-redemption is the rejection of biblical ethical norms and the promotion of the distortion of biblical sexuality (see below, "Sexuality: Spiritual and Physical Androgyny").

CHRISTOLOGY: CHRIST OUR TWIN BROTHER

My friend Jim is an identical twin. Once he went to the airport to meet his brother who was arriving from Europe after an absence of a few years. As they met they both burst out laughing. They were wearing identical clothing—the same colored slacks, the same style of jacket, and matching ties—proving once again that identical twins tend to be identical. Jim and his brother help us understand the Christology of the *Gospel of Thomas*.

Gospels tell about the events of Christ's birth, life, death, and space-time resurrection—right? Not this one. In the *Gospel of Thomas*, as generally in the other Gnostic gospels, there is no interest in history. The so-called "living Jesus" is simply there, an ethereal figure in no place or time in particular, revealing 114 wisdom sayings (*logia*). All this comes down to saying that there is no interest in the specific person of the flesh-and-bones historical man, Jesus Christ. Even the expression of Paul regarding the risen Christ, "that I might know him,"[21] is a sentiment largely unknown in Gnostic literature. Christ is merely a symbol of full consciousness and self-knowledge.

Essentially what Christ reveals is that the Gnostic is also a Christ. This is the implicit teaching right from the opening verse: "These are the secret words which the living Jesus spoke, and which Didymus [the twin] Judas Thomas wrote." In the canonical Gospels (Matt. 16:16ff., etc.), Jesus elicits from his disciples the confession, "You are the Christ." In the *Gospel of Thomas* the living Jesus confesses that the disciples are Christs. The canonical narrative of Peter's confession is reproduced for ridicule. It remains on a superficial level of understanding, and is thus marginalized, as the following saying shows:

> Jesus said to his disciples: "Make me a comparison; tell me what I am like." Simon Peter [representing orthodox misunderstanding] said to him: "You are like a righteous angel." Matthew [also representing orthodoxy] said to him: "You are like a man who is a wise philosopher." Thomas [the true Gnostic] said to him: "Master, my mouth will not be capable of saying what you are like." Jesus said [to Thomas]: "I am not your master, because you drank from the bubbling stream which I have measured out. . . ."[22]

Thomas comes to comprehend that he is the spiritual equal of Jesus, his identical twin brother, no less. Thomas is thus the true apostle whom every true Gnostic must follow.[23] If he is the twin brother of Jesus, so are they. The *Testimony of Truth* speaks of the Gnostic as one who becomes a "disciple of his own mind,"[24] equal to everyone, and independent of everyone. So "whoever achieves gnosis becomes 'no longer a Christian, but a Christ.'"[25] Similarly, in the *Dialog of the Savior,* the disciples ask, "What is the place to which we shall go?" The Savior answers, ". . . the place you can reach, stand there!" This is comparable to the phrase in the *Gospel of Thomas* (logion 24 [38.5-10]), "There is light within a man of light." According to Pagels, "Both sayings direct one . . . to oneself—to one's inner capacity to find one's own direction, to the 'light within.'"[26]

Beyond the reduction of Christology to the common religious experience of all believers, Gnosticism goes one malevolent step further. As we have seen, the *Testimony of Truth,* (49.7), after describing the serpent according to the Ophite reversal, adds, "For this is Christ."[27] So, in ancient Gnosticism we witness the ultimate blasphemy of Satanist distortion. Christ, the Son of God is the serpent.

THEOLOGY: GOD, THE UNKNOWABLE AND THE IMPERSONAL

The true God, according to the Gnostic, is strictly unknowable, without personality, and un-

28

touched by the world. God is but the ground of existence and is only known by the divine spark in mankind. No anthropomorphic element can ultimately be predicated of deity. Nevertheless Elaine Pagels,[28] in her book *The Gnostic Gospels,* has a chapter on the Gnostic idea of God entitled, "God the Father/God the Mother." She notes that while the God of Israel shared his power with no female deity, that was not the case for the Gods of the ancient Near East. In the Gnostic God there is a dyad of masculine and feminine elements, a dynamic relationship of opposites like the *yin* and the *yang.*[29]

The *Apocalypse of Adam* tells of a feminine power that becomes androgynous or lesbian, and, in the *Trimorphic Protennoia* found at Nag Hammadi, the divine feminine revealer cries:

> I am androgynous. [I am both Mother and] Father since I [copulate] with myself. I [copulate] with myself [and with those who love] me, [and] it is through me alone that the All [stands firm]. I am the Womb [that gives shape] to the All by giving birth to the Light that [shines in] splendor. I am the Aeon to [come. I am] the fulfillment of the All, that is . . . the glory of the Mother. (45.2-4)

Pagels refers to some Gnostic texts where God the Creator is castigated by a higher, feminine power, Sophia, and so comes to recognize, from the shock of this reality, that "the fear of the Lord is the beginning of wisdom."[30] The feminization of God led directly to the ordination of women.

This theology had immediate practical consequences in the ancient church. The early Gnostic, Marcion, excommunicated from the Roman Church in A.D. 150, established his own church, in which he appointed women as bishops and priests. In Valentinian Gnosticism women functioned as teachers, evangelists, healers, priests, and perhaps as bishops.[31]

In sum, Gnosticism rejected the Creator God of Scripture as blind, envious, and malicious, not hesitating to commit the most heinous blasphemy of all, which was to call him the Devil.[32] For the Gnostic, the true God was an unknowable, impersonal force, the unified sum of all the separated parts. In anthropology and sexuality, (see the following section) the divine being is thus best expressed by androgyny, that is, the erasure of the male-female distinction.

SEXUALITY: SPIRITUAL AND PHYSICAL ANDROGYNY

I know I have your attention for this section! We have all been raised in the sexually obsessive culture of the twentieth century. Among other things, we tend to think that the public discussion, display, and acceptance of sex—especially deviant sex, is unique to our time, a social phenomenon produced by Hollywood's grasp for filthy lucre and the hippie sexual revolution of the sixties. As in other domains, history teaches us that there is nothing new.

Gnosticism shares with ancient Greek philosophy a denigration of the physical body as an expression of the cosmic gaffe that produced the material creation. The body (*soma*) is thus seen as the prison-house (*sema*) of the soul (*pneuma*). Death is the setting free of the soul, and anything prior to death that undermines the body's materiality, anything that relativizes creation's hold, is thought to be a step in the right direction. Pagels notes that in the Valentinian system:

> It is not God but the demiurge who reigns as king and lord, who acts as military commander, who gives the law and judges those who violate it. . . . through the initiation Valentinus offers, the candidate learns to reject the creator's authority. . . . Achieving gnosis involves coming to recognize the true source of divine power . . . the depth of all being. . . . Whoever comes to this gnosis . . . is ready to receive the sacrament of redemption, i.e., release. . . . In this ritual he addresses the demiurge, declaring his independence, serving notice that he no longer belongs to the demiurge's sphere of authority and judgment.[33]

One of the Gnostic self-designations, reported by Hippolytus[34] is "the generation without a king" (*he abasileutos genea*), or "the undominated generation,"[35] by which "they declare themselves independent of any authority, human or divine."[36]

This autonomous anticreational theology has immediate practical effects in the area of sexuality. In this regard the last logion, number 114, of the *Gospel of Thomas* is of great interest. As the last it doubtless represents the goal of this gospel's teaching. It holds out for the believer the attainment of an androgynous or sexless state.

> Simon Peter said to them: "Let Mary go away from us, for women are not worthy of life." Jesus said: "Lo, I shall lead her, so that I may make her a male, that she too may become a living spirit, resembling you males. For every woman who makes herself a male will enter the kingdom of heaven."

According to Bertil Gaertner, an early authority on this gospel, logion 114 should be understood in the light of logion 22, which reads,

> And when you make the male and the female into a single one so that the male shall not be male and the female shall not be female . . . then you shall enter the kingdom.

Both these logia suggest, according to Gaertner, the "neutralization" of sexuality so that the ideal for Gnostics is to become sexless.[37] Whatever else these logia mean, they certainly contain, as is to be expected, a radical refusal of sexual differentiation, and a confusion of sexual identity. Behind these sayings is the classic Gnostic refusal of creational sexuality as presented in the Genesis account.[38] The diabolically inspired role reversal associated with the Fall is now lauded in Gnosticism as the path to redemption. The serpent and the woman are the "teachers."[39] The Creator and Adam are fools. The inversion of sexual roles leads to sexual confusion. Since the evil and foolish Creator is male, and true divinity is androgynous, it follows that the true Gnostic will finally seek androgyny. This was argued in particular by two Gnostic teachers, Marcus and Theodotus,[40] and was the starting point of knowledge of the Gnostic Naasenes, according to the church father Hippolytus.[41] These worshipers of the serpent also believed, against the Genesis account, that the original Adam was an hermaphrodite, appealing to Galatians 3:28, which they understood to say that the new creature, neither male nor female, is an hermaphrodite.[42] Whatever Galatians 3:28 says, it certainly does not say, "In Christ believers are *both* male and female"![43]

TECHNIQUES FOR SELF-KNOWING: GOING WITHIN

Hints of such techniques are found in some of the documents discovered at Nag Hammadi. In *Zostrianos* the author sets out a program that others are to follow, including ascetic practices and meditation to reduce "chaos in the mind," and by which he receives a first vision of the divine presence. After being deeply troubled he sees a vision of "the messenger of the knowledge of eternal Light." The *Discourse on the Eighth and Ninth* discloses the nine levels of knowledge through which the adept Gnostic must ascend in order to commune with the perfect invisible God. The master then leads the disciple in a prayer-chant of vowels and nonsense words: "Zoxathazo a oo ee ooo eee oooo ee ooooooooooo ooooo uuuuu ooooooooooo ooo

Zozazoth."[44] There follows an ecstatic state and a vision of the divine mediated through the master. The *Discourse* closes as the master instructs the student to write his experience in a book to guide others who will "advance by stages, and enter into the way of immortality . . . into the understanding of the eighth that reveals the ninth."[45]

Few accounts of these techniques have survived in written form since the Gnostics followed the secrecy patterns of the Greco-Roman mystery religions. Enough, however, is divulged in this one text, and implied in others, to reveal how central such techniques are to the entire system. As we shall see in the case of the New Age, self-knowledge is impossible without self-exploration. Only by penetrative self-meditation can the adept seem to rise above the restraints of body and cosmic materiality. Only by such experimentation can believers "know"— that is, "experience"—that they are divine.

SUMMARY

This rapid overview of ancient Gnosticism reveals a diabolically inspired and profoundly coherent system of beliefs despite great diversity and apparent disunity. It was a system dedicated to the overthrow of orthodox Christianity by means of (1) the rejection of God the Creator and the destruction of the creational structures, especially those concerning sexual identity, and (2) the distortion of the Christian message of redemption by the eradication of the concept of sin, and the dehistoricizing and spiritualizing of Christology and salvation. In this way Christ becomes a symbol of every Gnostic believer, and redemption is the fruit of one's own efforts to gain transforming knowledge that one is God.

Are there strong ties between this ancient system of belief—apparently defunct for centuries—and the contemporary religious phenomenon now called the New Age? Read on.

NOTES

1. Breakfast cereal is not even on offer in present-day Russia, according to our Russian house-guest.

2. This list was taken at random from the local New Age newspaper, *The Light Connection*, July, 1992.

3. Acts 17:16-33. While it is true that Paul was "greatly distressed to see that the city was full of idols," the variety of idolatrous methods no doubt boggled his mind.

4. Kurt Rudolph, *Gnosis: The Nature and History of an Ancient Religion* (Edinburgh: T. and T. Clark, 1983), 9, 53.

5. Ibid., 57.

6. *Hypostasis of the Archons* 89.30-35, cited by Karen L. King, "Ridicule and Rape, Rule and Rebellion," in *Gnosticism and the Early Christian World*, ed. James E. Goehring, Charles W. Hedrick, Jack T. Sanders with Hans Dieter Betz (Sonoma, Calif.: Polebridge Press, 1990), 9.

7. Orval Wintermute, "Gnostic Exegesis of the Old Testament," in J. M. Efird, ed., *The Use of the Old Testament in the New and Other Essays* (Durham, N.C.: Duke University Press, 1972), 257.

8. Ibid., 258.

9. *Apocalypse of Adam* 64.5-20; 85.20-30. See

Martin, "Genealogy and Sociology in the Apocalypse of Adam," in Goehring, *Gnosticism and the Early Christian World*, 34.

10. *Hypostasis of the Archons* 89.30-35, cited by Wintermute, "Gnostic Exegesis of the Old Testament," 252, shows that this was justified by assigning the Aramaic meaning ("instructor") to the Hebrew word HYH, "wild animal," of which the serpent was one (Gen. 3:1).

11. Cited in ibid., 259 n. 23. See also the treatment of this theme by Birger A. Pearson, *Gnosticism, Judaism, and Egyptian Christianity* (Minneapolis: Augsburg Fortress, 1990), 43ff., a publication of the Institute for Antiquity and Christianity. In the *Testimony of Truth* the Coptic term describing the wisdom of the serpent is stronger than that used in the Bible and means "revealer of wisdom and knowledge." In this literature the serpent is the "instructor" of Eve, and Eve is the "instructor" of Adam (see *On the Origin of the Worlds* 113:33; cp. the *Hypostasis of the Archons* 89.32; 90.6). Gnosticism clearly makes the role reversals and role confusion an aspect of wisdom.

In this same document the serpent-instructor is called "the beast" (*therion;* see 114.3), in this context a title of nobility. Revelation uses this term for a being who is the embodiment of evil (11:7), whom the inhabitants of the earth will worship, and who will make war against the saints and conquer them (13:7). His bestial successor is given the number 666 (13:18).

12. Irenaeus, *Against Heresies* 1.27.3 (see Alexander Roberts and James Donaldson, *The Anti-Nicene Fathers* [Grand Rapids: Eerdmans, 1971], 1:352), suggests that Marcion believed the serpent possessed him. Marcion believed in the salvation brought by the serpent, by which Cain, the men of Sodom, and the Egyptians were saved while Abel, Enoch, Noah, Abraham, and the prophets perished. Irenaeus also recounts a tradition concerning a meeting between Polycarp and Marcion. The latter asked, "Do you know us?" and Polycarp answered, "I know you, the first born of Satan" (*Against Heresies* 3.3.3).

Hippolytus gives an extended treatment of the Naasenes, who worship the serpent. Their doctrines are classically Gnostic, as for example their rejection of the Old Testament and of the sacrificial system. "The universal serpent is . . . the wise discourse of Eve. . . . this is the mark that was set upon Cain that anyone who findeth him might not kill him. This . . . is Cain, whose sacrifice the god of this world did not accept. The gory sacrifice, however, of Abel he approved of; for the ruler of this world rejoices in blood" (*Refutation of All Heresies,* xl). See also the discussions in H. Jonas, *The Gnostic Religion* (Boston: Beacon Press, 1963), 92-95, and Rudolph, *Gnosis,* 84ff.

13. Irenaeus, *Against Heresies* 5.26.2, cited in Elaine Pagels, *The Gnostic Gospels* (New York: Random House, 1981), 53.

14. *Refutation of All Heresies* 5.6-17. Hippolytus's witness has been confirmed by the discovery of the Nag Hammadi texts. Note also that the "Cainite" Gnostics adopted "Ophite" worship (see Pearson, *Gnosticism,* 96ff. In general, the serpent's reputation as wily allowed it to be seen as a symbol for wisdom. Its twisting coils "suggested the perpetual revolution of the universe and the cosmic power that moves it," according to *The Oxford Dictionary of the Christian Church,* 2d ed., ed. F. L. Cross (New York: Oxford University Press, 1983), 1000-1001.

The serpent, because of its phallic symbolism, is often associated with sexuality, especially in Hinduism. This notwithstanding, the Naasenes, according to the account of Hippolytus, eschewed sexual intercourse with a women and practiced a form of emasculation. Then Hippolytus's account immediately goes on: "And they do not worship any other object but Naas . . . the serpent from whom, i.e., from the word Naas, . . . are all that under heaven are denominated temples (Naos). . . . And these [Naasenes] affirm that the serpent is a moist substance . . . and that nothing of existing things . . . could consist at all without him" (5.4). All this is subsumed by Hippolytus under what the Naasenes call the "mysteries of

the 'Great Mother.'" One cannot help but wonder whether between the lines there is not suggested in the matrix of emas-
culated men, a great mother, and the worship of a phallic symbol a form of (spiritual?) homosexuality. This has been suggested for "Sethian" Gnosticism by A. Boehlig and F. Wisse,
*Nag Hammadi Codices III, 2 and IV, 2: The Gospel of the
Egyptians* (NHS 4; Leiden: Brill, 1975), 35. See also Pearson,
Gnosticism, 80. Such practices would only be hinted at by ancient texts, as is indicated by the comment of Irenaeus about
the "Cainite gnostics": "Others say that Cain was from the superior power, and confess Esau and Korah and the Sodomites
and all such as their kinsmen. . . . I have also collected writings of theirs, in which they urge the destruction of the works
of Hystera (the womb) [normal sexual intercourse and child-
bearing?]; Hystera is the name they give to the fabricator of
heaven and earth. And they say they cannot be saved in any
other way, except they pass through all things. . . . And at
every sinful and base action an angel is present and instills in
him who ventures the deed audacity and impurity. . . . And
this is the perfect 'knowledge,' to enter without fear into such
operations, which it is not lawful even to name" (*Against
Heresies* 1.31.1-2).

15. Pearson, *Gnosticism,* 132.

16. Cited in Groothuis, *Jesus,* 83.

17. See *The Nag Hammadi Library in English* (San
Francisco: Harper and Row, 1977), 409.

18. Pearson, *Gnosticism,* 133.

19. Bertil Gaertner, *The Theology of the Gospel of Thomas*
(New York: Harper, 1961), 21, 213, emphasizes the polemic
character of this text.

20. *Gospel of Thomas,* 32.19-33.5

21. Phil. 3:10.

22. *Gospel of Thomas,* 34.31-35.7.

23. Pagels, *Gnostic Gospels,* 157.

24. The *Testimony of Truth* 44:2.

25. *Gospel of Philip,* 67.26-27.

26. Pagels, *Gnostic Gospels,* 144.

27. Pearson, *Gnosticism,* 50. The ancient Gnostic looked within and saw Christ, the serpent. How far, in actual fact, is this from the New Age Hindu-inspired *kundalini* meditation, where the kundalini (i.e., serpent or life force) is raised from the base chakra to the crown chakra, in a sort of self-induced penetration by the serpent? See MacLaine, *Going Within,* 193-94. This question is speculative because the documents are not very explicit on these issues.

28. *Gnostic Gospels,* 57ff.

29. Ibid., 61.

30. Ibid., 69-70.

31. See ibid., 72.

32. Pearson, *Gnosticism,* 48, refers to the Gnostic use of the name "Samael," "the blind god" or "the god of the blind," to refer to the God of the Bible, a name Judaism applied to the Devil (see 2 Cor. 4:4). Another etymology associates Samael with the "accuser," which again is a term for the Devil (Rev. 12:10). On page 92 Pearson does not shrink back from the following conclusion: "The Gnostic author of this document [*The Hypostasis of the Archons*] has thus equated YHWH, who declares his sole Deity in Isa. 43:11 . . . with the devil."

33. Pagels, *Gnostic Gospels,* 44.

34. *Refutation of All Heresies* 5.8.2.

35. See Pearson, *Gnosticism,* 132-33 for the terms in Coptic, and references to the Nag Hammadi literature. Pearson shows that the Gnostics share with the highest God his attributes, and their conception of total freedom corresponds to the definition of the primal Father as "the Monad [who] is a monarchy with nothing above it" (*Apocryphon of John* 2.2.26-27).

36. Ibid.

37. Gaertner, *The Theology of the Gospel of Thomas,* 256.

38. For a careful exegesis of Gen. 1-3, see Raymond C. Ortland, Jr., "Male-Female Equality and Male Headship: Gen. 1-3," in *Recovering Biblical Manhood and Womanhood,* ed. J. Piper and W. Grudem (Wheaton, Ill.: Crossway Books, 1991), 95-112.

39. Pearson, *Gnosticism*, 44: "The serpent's role as 'teacher' is underscored in the interchange between God, Eve and Adam [in the *Testimony of Truth* 47.1-4], where it is stated that the woman 'instructed' Adam, and the serpent had 'instructed' the woman. Indeed the teaching role of both the serpent and Eve is the subject of considerable speculation in Gnostic literature." On this see Elaine Pagels, *Adam, Eve and the Serpent* (New York: Random House, 1988), 66-70. Paul's instruction concerning sexual roles in the church is especially interesting in the light of this Gnostic inversion of the Genesis account. "A woman should learn in quietness and full submission. I do not permit a woman to teach or to have authority over a man; she must be silent. For Adam was formed first, then Eve. And Adam was not the one deceived; it was the woman who was deceived and became a sinner. But women will be saved through childbearing—if they continue in faith, love and holiness with propriety" (1 Tim. 2:11-15).

It would appear that one has here an inverted mirror image of the same text, or, to put it differently, two diametrically opposed exegeses of the same text. In Paul, Adam is first, then Eve; in the *Testimony of Truth*, Eve is given first place, and Adam follows along. In Paul, the man teaches (*didaskein*) while the woman learns in willful submission; in *Testimony of Truth* the woman teaches (*tcabo* [Coptic]) and the man submits to her teaching. In Paul the woman is deceived by the serpent; in *Testimony of Truth* she is enlightened by the serpent. In Paul the woman gives life through child-bearing; in *Testimony of Truth* she gives life through her instruction (47.1)—cp. the heavenly Eve, "Instructor of Life" who comes into the serpent, also called the "instructor" (the *Hypostasis of the Archons* 113.33; cp. 89.32; 90.6, cited by Pearson, *Gnosticism*, 45). In Paul woman is saved by accepting the creational structures of marriage and child-bearing; in *Testimony of Truth* marriage and child-bearing are the evidence that one is still carnal, held under the law of Moses, like the scribes and Pharisees (50:1-5; 58:1; 68:5). For an excellent description of the Gnostic reinterpretation of Gen. 1-3, see R. C.

Kroeger and C. C. Kroeger, *I Suffer Not a Woman* (Grand Rapids: Baker, 1992), 117-77. The great insights of this study concerning Paul's biblical answer to Gnostic distortions is vitiated by the authors' rejection of this answer as applying only to an extreme, first-century situation. The authors fail to see that this same Gnostic heresy is back with a vengeance via the New Age teaching seeping into the contemporary church and society, and that Paul's teaching has perhaps never been more relevant than now.

40. See Pagels, *Gnostic Gospels,* 67.

41. *Refutation of All Heresies* 5.1.

42. *Refutation of All Heresies* 5.2.

43. For then one would be obliged to argue that Christians were both Jews and Greeks, slaves and free, which is nonsense.

44. See also the *Gospel of the Egyptians,* "the holy book of the Great Invisible Spirit . . . i.e., the great Seth," which reveals the imperishable name: "Ie ieus eo ou eo oua! Really truly, O Yessus Mazareus Yessedekeus, O living water, O child of the child, O glorious name, really, truly, aion o on, iiii eeee eeee oo oo uuuu oooo aaaa{a}, really, truly, ei aaaa oooo, O existing one who sees the aeons! Really, truly, aee eee iiii uu-uuuu ooooooo, who is eternally eternal, really, truly, iea aio, in the heart, who exists, u aei eis aei, ei o ei, eo os ei. . . . Thou art what Thou art, Thou art who Thou art!" (*Nag Hammadi Library,* 204). Pearson, *Gnosticism,* 77, shows a deep relationship between the *Gospel of the Egyptians* and *Zostrianos.*

45. All of this material is cited from Pagels, *Gnostic Gospels,* 165.

4

The New Age—The Return of Ancient Gnosticism

OUT OF IGNORANCE INTO UNDERSTANDING

It was four o'clock in the afternoon. The room temperature was high, the atmosphere heavy. My afternoon nap, already two hours overdue, threatened to overpower me. I was anxiously aware of my lowering resistance. The professor, an otherwise likable chap, droned on about "ogdoads" and "aeons." He began to read from *The Tripartate Tractate:*

> The one whom he took up as a light for those who came from himself, the one from whom they take their name, he is the Son, who is full, complete, and blameless. He brought him forth united with the one who came forth from him partaking of the glory from the totality, in so far as each one can receive him for himself, since his greatness is not such before they receive him, but he does certainly exist, as

he is in his own manner and form and greatness.
. . .[1]

By the time he reached the third sentence, I
was gone. Sleep rolled over me like a London fog.
Basking in a world of private glory, I was about to
make my second consecutive hole-in-one in the final round of the Masters' Golf Championship at the
Augusta National when I hit the floor. The resulting embarrassment was my only emotional involvement with this ancient, apparently extinct, religious
movement.

The course on Gnosticism, a requirement for
my New Testament doctoral program in the late sixties, was boring and far removed from my Christian
faith and my day-to-day concerns. Few were talking
of the New Age Movement.

Since that time, my mind has been radically
changed. Recently I have discovered that New Age
religion and Gnosticism, separated by some fifteen
hundred years, nevertheless resemble one another
like two Siamese cats, sometimes even to the small-
est detail. This seems incredible. Should not an ancient, mythological system have disappeared forever
as mankind has constantly evolved into the intelligent, nonsuperstitious, rational, scientific beings we
know today? While a few New Age thinkers consider
scientific humanism's two-hundred-year program of
rational criticism as itself a myth that needs to be
and is being replaced, we may still wonder what ancient Gnosticism could possibly have to do with the
religious aspirations of a growing number of so-

phisticated and intelligent people at the end of the twentieth century. The answer is, pretty much everything. Furthermore, this pagan system, in both its ancient and modern forms, represents the very antithesis of true Christianity. Understanding the lie is of utmost importance for comprehending the truth. Like all heresies, this one will provoke the contemporary church to sharpen its understanding of orthodoxy, thereby enhancing its witness in the specific struggles of its own day.

If I bore my readers the way my professor bored me with his study of ancient Gnosticism, I humbly apologize. The time is not for boredom but for action. As our world nears the mysterious year of 2000,[2] the church must wake from its dreams of glory to confront the reality of a new Gnostic invasion. Understanding what the New Age prophets are teaching at the end of the twentieth century is a requirement, not just for doctoral students but for all Christians who desire to serve Christ in our time.

COSMOLOGY: LET US WORSHIP THE GREAT GREEN ONE

The New Age seems to have progressed far beyond the old Gnostic rejection of the material world. Linked to the present concerns for ecology, attention has recently turned to the development of a "creation spirituality," often under the Christian label. Apparently one New Age United Presbyterian minister in Colorado, during the Sunday service, prayed to "the great Green One."[3] Her royal greenness turns out to be the goddess Gaia, Mother Earth, who gives to the universe its basic unity. Christian liturgies beg her forgiveness using Hindu chants to channel her life-giving energy. Though the word "creation" is used, it is given a totally different meaning than that of the biblical concept. There is no real interest in creation. There is no creation account. The word is simply another way of referring to the sum of all things, understood according to syncretistic pantheism. For this way of thinking, the biblical concept of God the Creator distinct from his creation, creating *ex nihilo* (from nothing) is abhorrent. Indeed, this God—a phallic, vengeful, sadistic Deity, a God of guilt—has to go, according to Matthew Fox, a Dominican New Age theologian.[4] Radical religious feminism promotes witchcraft as the most direct way to goddess Nature worship. Miriam Starhawk, a leader of this movement does not see the goddess as external to the world. "She is the world. Manifest in each of us."[5] It follows that new-look feminist witchcraft is a religion of ecology.[6]

Clearly this earth-goddess worship has nothing to do with the biblical doctrine of creation. Indeed, another contradictory idea of creation dominates. Shirley MacLaine allies herself with Oriental thinking. Just as oriental thinking believed in the superiority of spirit over matter, so Western New Age thinking believes that, by the use of mental and spiritual powers, human beings can dominate the limitations that the physical imposes upon them and thus create themselves.[7] Hindu meditation on the second chakra reveals the following fundamental understanding: "The body is basically an aggregate of universal particles that one's Higher Self has sculpted to experience physical existence and truly fulfill its purpose for that life-time. When the mission is completed, the particles disperse and become part of the earth."[8] So, like Gnosticism, there is no given creational reality to which creatures must conform. "Creatures"—what an offensive term! We are rather co-creators, creating, like "God," our own spiritual reality. This is pro-choice ideology raised to the nth power! If murderous creativity sounds strange, it should!

Because physical existence is ultimately an illusion, a further common theme between Gnosticism and New Age thinking about the world is the general acceptance of reincarnation. The goal of New Age reincarnation, like that of the ancient Gnostic, is to be finally freed from the illusion of physical existence and the great wheel of karma and to be absorbed in the All.[9] So death, as in Gnosticism, is "the most complete and immediate means to the void."[10] In words that could have been lifted straight out of an ancient Gnostic text, Shirley MacLaine declares, "Birth into the physical is . . . a limitation of the spirit, and death of the physical is the return of the spirit to its proper domain."[11]

REDEMPTION: MIND OVER MATTER, FEMALE OVER MALE

In *The Silver Chair* C. S. Lewis introduced his young readers to the redoubtable Lady of the Green

Kirtle, the Queen of Underland. This malefic female sought by enchantments to convince the Narnians that the Overworld (true spiritual reality) is but a figment of their imagination and that the only real world is her dark and evil kingdom. However, when cornered by the truth, the Witch-queen's form began to alter.

> Her arms appeared to be fastened to her sides. Her legs were intertwined with each other, and her feet . . . disappeared. The long green train of her skirt thickened and grew solid, and seemed to be of one piece with the writhing green pillar of her interlocking legs. And that . . . green pillar was curving and swaying as if it had no joints. Her head was thrown far back and while her nose grew longer and longer, every other part of her face seemed to disappear, except her eyes. Huge flaming eyes they were now, without brows or lashes.[12]

The beautiful woman became a writhing venomous serpent.

Malevolent female power is not just the fare of children's story books. Today it is an essential element of Aquarian eschatology. The ultimate incarnation of antichrist may well be a woman!

The Goddess Savior. As for the Gnostic, so in contemporary New Age thinking, the female principle holds the key to salvation. James Lovelock, a New Age spokesman, calls for a return to goddess spirituality to avoid the destruction to which the Semitic/Christian God will inevitably lead.[13] Shirley

MacLaine dedicates her book *Going Within* to "Sachi, Mother, Kathleen and Bella and all the other women *and* men who seek the spiritual feminine in themselves." So the common lines reappear after fifteen centuries. Karen L. King, in commenting on the use of gender language in the ancient Gnostic text *Hypostasis of the Archons,* notes the employment of feminine language to represent both the savior and the Gnostic believer. Norea, the female savior, is "strong and present. She is the source of life and teaching."[14] The Jewish feminist theologian Rita Gross advocates the borrowing from Hindu goddess traditions in order to effect the "second coming of the goddess."[15] Indeed, in Hindu Saktism the goddess is the savior.[16]

Much of radical feminism is borne along by a mythology of the woman as savior. The essential myth, masquerading as history, (and denounced as such by feminist archaeologist Joan B. Townsend[17]) sees a past golden age that was matriarchal, matrilocal, and matrilineal. God was in fact a goddess, peace reigned, and women were equal with or superior to men. This idyllic society was overthrown by male-dominated war-like societies worshiping male gods, hence our present problems of crime, drugs, immorality, greed, and wars of destruction. Says Townsend in her description of this thinking:

> If society is to be saved and world destruction avoided . . . it remains for women to reinstate the Goddess worship in order to establish equal reli-

49

gious rights and socio-political positions of equality with men, if not dominance. . . . The goddess forms a ritual focus around which women can identify and unify to save all of us from destruction and bring about the millennium . . . the peace and harmony of control by women.[18]

The Serpent Savior. The Naasenes (the ancient Gnostic worshipers of the serpent) are roaming the land again. Already Madame Blavasky, who died in 1891, but whose writings are held in high esteem in the New Age Movement, attributed redemption to Satan.

The appellation Satan . . . and "Adversary" belongs by right to the first and cruelest "Adversary" of all other gods—Jehovah; not to the serpent which spoke only words of sympathy and wisdom. . . . The Great Serpent of the Garden of Eden and the "Lord God" are identical. . . . Satan, the serpent . . . is the real creator and benefactor, the Father of spiritual mankind. For it is he who opened the eyes of Adam.[19]

Today the worship of Satan is no longer the province of esoteric or marginal thinkers. Today's version is brought to you courtesy of a main-line Lutheran printing house, Augsburg Fortress Publications. Anne Primavesi's *From Apocalypse to Genesis* (1991) is offered as "a profound and original re-evaluation of Christianity."[20] Genesis is reread via a radical questioning of the notions of original sin, redemption, and salvation, by showing that the "the story of 'Eve'[21] should be read not as that of the 'Fall' of the human race, but of its coming to maturity"![22] Is not that exactly what Satan has always wanted people to think? And when you have said that, the old, blatant, blasphemous, ophistic (serpent-worshiping) themes are not long in making their appearance. The serpent, our "Christian" eco-feminist theologian assures us, is "the symbol of wisdom offered to humankind. . . . expos[ing] the problem of keeping rules. . . . [teaching that] any rules . . . even supposedly divine codes . . . which operate as rules of helplessness *must be resisted.*"[23] As in Gnosticism, the Creator God of Genesis, the foolish Demiurge, has to go. He is male, is tyrannical, denies basic human liberties, demands total obedience, and threatens punishment for evil deeds. Consequently original sin is not to be found in man but in God. The classic, orthodox Christian reading of Genesis, notes Primavesi, assumes God's actions "to be beyond reproach *even when patently they are not.*"[24] Another of Fortress Press's recent offerings, also presented as a "fresh . . . formulation of Christian theology," is Ninian Smart and Steven Konstantine, *Christian Systematic Theology in a World Context.* These so-called Christian theologians make the same move. Espousing "Process Theology" (which believes God is evolving along with the creation), the authors state: "We shall not duck the issue: . . . the Ultimate is responsible for the evil in nature as well as the good." This admission is possible because God is part of the evolving, imperfect cosmos and is not sovereign over creation. "The independence of creatures places some limitations on her style of action."[25]

This kind of theological reversal is so often these days the end result of a commitment to feminist ideology. Feminist liberation is true, and everything else can be jettisoned—traditional family values, biblical canonical authority, the wisdom and goodness of God the Creator, and the very definition of the source of evil. An expression of similar radical theology comes from an unexpected source—the scholarly British publication, the *Journal for the Study of the New Testament,* published at the University of Sheffield and known for its conservative, even "evangelical" leanings. Though some of the leading British Evangelical New Testament specialists are on the present editorial board, this has not deterred its present editor, Francis Watson, from publishing an article whose extreme feminist positions almost defy the imagination. In his analysis of the teaching on human sexuality and roles in Genesis 1-3 and its canonical treatment in Paul, he finds the biblical text (new and old) hopelessly patriarchal and hierarchical. Watson considers quite unconvincing (no doubt correctly) all attempts to save these texts by recovering between the lines a sort of pristine egalitarianism. He leaves the reader with what he judges the "more appropriate strategy"—"resistance." Such resistance would take the form of a "counter-reading," reading the text "defiantly 'against the grain.'" In practice, this would involve seeing "the serpent as liberator, Eve as heroine in her courageous quest for wisdom and the Lord God as a jealous tyrant concerned only with the preservation of his own prerogatives. *Such a reading was, of course, adopted within Gnosticism. . . ."*[26]

With this conscious adoption of ancient Gnostic exegesis in a highly regarded scholarly journal of classic Christian roots, one must surely concede that the Gnostic empire is undoubtedly and disturbingly striking back. Watson is asking us to throw over the God of the Bible in terms evocative of those employed by the author Anatole France. In his 1914 novel, *The Revolt of the Angels,* France proposes a similar Gnostic inversion of human salvation.

> The God of old is dispossessed of His terrestrial empire, and every thinking being on this globe disdains Him or knows Him not. But what matter that men should be no longer submissive to Ialdaboath [the Gnostic parody on Jahweh] if the spirit of Ialdaboath is still in them; if they, like Him, are jealous, violent, quarrelsome and greedy, and the foes of the arts and beauty? What matter that they have rejected the ferocious demiurge? It is in ourselves and in ourselves alone the we must attack and destroy Ialdaboath.[27]

To bring this call to deicide up-to-date, one need only add to the list of "foes" the foes of feminist liberation. Especially in the church, this appears to be the tail wagging the dog of a neo-Gnostic revision of Christianity (see "Sexuality," below). But the bottom line defies belief. As with ancient Gnosticism, the goal of liberation and the denunciation of oppression produces a total reversal of values. This so-called new-look "Christian" theology, in its extreme but logical expression, defiantly pulls the biblical God of Creation and redemption from his throne and puts him to death on the altar of egalitarianism. Human redemption is achieved at the price of death—not the death of Christ on the Cross, but the assassination of God, the Creator of heaven and earth. At the same time that old Serpent, masquerading as "liberator" and "illuminator," slithers up the royal steps to take command.[28]

Ex-Christian fundamentalist David Spangler, a contemporary spokesman of the New Age, speaks of a coming "Luciferic initiation." "Lucifer works within each of us to bring us wholeness as we move into the New Age. . . . Lucifer comes to give us the final . . . Luciferic initiations . . . that many people in the days ahead will be facing, for it is an initiation into the New Age."[29] Like the Gnostic *Apocryphon of John,* in which Jesus tells Adam and Eve to eat of the tree of the knowledge of good and evil, so Spangler says, "Christ is the same force as Lucifer"; Lucifer prepares man for Christ-consciousness. The ultimate identification of Christ with Satan is a natural outcome of monism (all is one, one is all). Both good and evil are equally part of the whole. Thus the proto-New Ager of the sixties, Charles Manson, led his follows in the bloody massacre of Sharon Tate and her friends, believing that everything he did was "good," an expression of karma. For this reason his followers saw him as both Satan and Christ.[30]

The Self-Savior. The way to this new consciousness is inward, not in order to recognize one's sin, but to discover how good and powerful—literally, how divine—one is.[31] "I found God in myself and I loved her fiercely," says Roman Catholic theologian Carol Christ.[32] As does the Gnostic, the New Age believer identifies the real human problem as ignorance. But "a great awakening is taking place," says Shirley MacLaine. "Individuals across the world are tapping in to their internal power to understand who they are and using that knowledge to elevate their lives and their circumstances to a higher octave of happiness and productivity."[33] (Is not this the very essence of the original temptation offered to Eve?) They are tapping in to their higher self. The good news is that the higher self is constituted by "the best positive elements of your own being, the most reassuring aspect of your inner strength, your personal expression of the divine in you."[34] In the light of this, notice how modern the ancient Gnostic, Monoimus, sounds:

> Abandon the search for God and the creation and other matters of a similar sort. Look for him by taking yourself as the starting point. Learn who it is within you who makes everything his own and says, "My god, my mind, my thought, my soul, my body." Learn the sources of sorrow, joy, love, hate. . . . If you carefully investigate these matters you will find him in yourself.[35]

There is a strange ring of the old Gnostic New Age spirituality in certain forms of modern Christianity. Smart and Konstantine speak of "a Divine Being who lies within and beyond the cosmos . . . but we also find the Divine within us, at the base of our consciousness. In searching inside ourselves *through self-training* we can find her in the Light which lights our consciousness."[36]

The Superfluous Savior. The acquisition of self-knowledge allows no concept of sin. As the Voice (supposedly Jesus)[37] that possessed Dr. Helen Schucman, a Jewish atheist and psychologist in 1965, explained, in *A Course in Miracles,* evil is an illusion, and sin is the illusion that separates us from our own innate divinity, our own godhood.[38] This voice of Jesus soothingly intones, "Forget your dreams of sin and guilt and come with me," and then goes on quite naturally to deny the reality of the Cross. Because there is no sin, Jesus Christ as Savior becomes superfluous. In classic Gnostic conceptuality this Jesus declares, "It is impossible to kill the Son of God."[39] Elizabeth Clare Prophet, leader of the Church Universal and Triumphant, considered the idea of blood-sacrifice an "erroneous doctrine" of dubious pagan origin.[40] Matthew Fox sees Jesus' death as a symbol of Mother Earth dying each day as a constantly sacrificed paschal lamb. What an utter confusion between the once-for-all dealing with sin in Christ's death and resurrection and the pagan cyclical notion of the rites of spring! In a similar vein, the New Age spiritualizes and explains away the resurrection and the ascension of Christ. Just as Rudolf Bultmann, the radical New Testament critic, claimed that Jesus was raised in the faith of the disciples, Joseph Campbell, in *The Power of Myth,* explains the ascension to mean that Christ "has gone inward . . . to the kingdom of heaven within."[41]

CHRISTOLOGY: CHRIST, A SPIRITUAL STATE, NOT A PERSON

In the New Age *Aquarian Gospel of Jesus Christ,* it is clearly stated:

> Jesus was not always Christ. Jesus won his Christship by a strenuous life, and in . . . chapter 55 we have a record of the events of his christing, or receiving the degree Christ. . . . We recognize the facts that Jesus was a man and that Christ was God. . . . Jesus is the flesh-made messenger to show that light to men. . . . But in the ages yet to come, man will attain to greater heights, and lights still more intense will come. And then, at last, a mighty master soul will come to earth to light the way up to the throne of perfect man.[42]

Since there is no unique redemptive work of Christ, he becomes merely a cipher and a symbol of the true believer. Schucman's *A Course in Miracles* reveals not only that Christ is our elder brother, who has gone on before, but also that we are his equals, being already perfect like him. How close this is to the ancient Gnostic text, the *Gospel of Thomas,* where the "living Jesus" teaches Thomas that he is not his master, but rather his twin brother.[43] Jesus

merely tapped into the cosmic Christ-consciousness, but we are all, according to Joseph Campbell,
"manifestations of Buddha consciousness, of Christ
consciousness, only we do not know it."[44] Like the
old Gnostics who disparaged the historical Jesus,
Primavesi, along with the film *The Last Temptation,*
makes Jesus into a sinner.[45]

And yet, Christ is the higher self. For Shirley
MacLaine:

> Christ demonstrated what we would call today pre-
> cognition, prophecy, levitation, telepathy and occult
> healing. But many others, before Christ and since,
> have demonstrated those same spiritual powers.
> They claim their powers come not only from God
> in "heaven" but from God within themselves con-
> necting with the superconsciousness.[46]

In New Age thinking Jesus really has no special
place. Like the Gnostic gospels, there is no interest
in the events of his birth, life, death, and resurrection. Orthodox Christianity is disparaged as a "Jesus
cult," whereas the New Age super-race possesses
"Christ consciousness."[47] This is stated quite bla-
tantly by New Ager, Hayward Cole.

> The right way of thinking is to see Christ in every
> human being. This may sound born again but it
> isn't. Born-again Christianity emphasizes the per-
> sonality of Jesus; what I call Christian Yoga sees
> Christ as a Consciousness.[48]

Irenaeus, were he alive today, would surely describe the New Age "Christology" as he described

ancient Gnosticism: "an abyss of madness and of blasphemy against Christ."[49]

THEOLOGY: "I AM GOD IN LIGHT"

"Fifty million Americans got the message: 'Hey, we are God.'" Such is one writer's estimation of the result of Shirley MacLaine's TV mini-series "Out on a Limb."[50] In her book the message is clearly stated.

> God lies within, and therefore we are each part of God. Since there is no separateness, we are each Godlike, and God is in each of us. . . . We are literally made up of God energy, therefore we can create whatever we want in life because we are each co-creating with the energy of God—the energy that makes the universe itself.[51]

This is a perfect example of pantheistic monism, which denies that God is the personal, unique Creator, distinct from creation. All is one and God is a cipher for the mass of energy that causes the universe to turn. This is practical atheism, for identifying God with everything, it effectively removes from God any real and specific identity. According to Matthew Fox the personal Creator and Redeemer God of the Bible is phallic and sadistic and must be jettisoned for the God within.[52]

The New Age God, like the God of Gnosticism, is impersonal and unknowable. Discovering oneself to be God, the Gnostic and the New Ager commit the same fundamental act of idolatry—the worship of the creature rather than the Creator. This ultimate inversion of the divine and the human in the spiritual realm produces perversion in the sexual realm, as Paul clearly shows in Romans 1:18-32.

SEXUALITY: THE NEW ANDROGYNOUS HUMANITY

When Shirley MacLaine goes within to gaze upon God (i.e., her higher self), she sees "a powerful form, quietly standing in the center of my inner space, looking at me with total love. The figure [is] very tall, an androgynous being with long arms and the kindest face . . . saying, 'I am the real you.'"[53] Thus each partner in relationships, both hetero- and homosexual, is encouraged to recognize the validity of both masculine and feminine, the *yang* and the *yin*, in himself or herself. We are coming out of the Piscean, masculine, *yang* age of left-brained intellectual reflection, declares MacLaine. We are now passing into the Aquarian age of *yin*, feminine energy of right-brained intuition and mystic spirituality.[54] "When the feminine goddess in each of us is recognized, the spiritualization of the physical plane will be accomplished. . . . Then we will have spiritualized the material. . . . and will be expressing ourselves . . . for what we truly are—androgynous, a perfect balance."[55] Modern religious feminism seeks to "move beyond God the Father 'to an imagery of bisexual androgynous deity by reintroducing the image of God as female to complement the image of God as male."[56] How close we are to ancient Gnosticism is indicated by the description, given by noted Italian Gnostic scholar Giovanni Filoramo, of the "androgynous god of the Gnostics," who expresses the "concept of *coniunction oppositorum,* or joining of opposites, to embody the conquest of all duality."[57] The road to this perfect androgynous balance involves the destruction of the traditional male-female differentiation via sexual alternatives and New Age feminism. The latter is expressed in New Age author Charlene Spretnak's book, *The Politics of Women's Spirituality,* published by Doubleday, the same publisher who brought you the Anchor Bible Commentary series.[58] This book is a call to bring to an end Judeo-Christian religion by a feminist movement nourished on goddess-worship paganism, and witchcraft that succeeds in overthrowing the global rule of men.[59]

Columnist William Grigg documents the growing attachment to goddess worship, and in the strangest of places. He cites in the *New York Times* an article that gives its imprimatur to this movement, accepting the myth that in ancient goddess-adoring matriarchies, "Life was peaceful, cooperative and egalitarian, while in societies focused on the male gods it was violent, authoritarian and stratified." The "pseudo-scholarship" of Monica Sjoo and Barbara Mor (*The Great Cosmic Mother*), Rosalind Miles (*The Women's History of the World*), and Riane Eisler (*The Chalice and the Blade*), creates the myth of an egalitarian goddess-based society that was destroyed by patriarchal usurpers. Grigg gauges the success of this movement by the sold-out performances and the rave

reviews in Mormon "patriarchal" Utah of the play
"Mother Wove the Morning," written by Carol Lynn
Pearson, herself a Mormon. In the play, Rachel, wife
of Jacob (Israel) remembers the benevolent era of the
goddess and the brutal, monotheist patriarchs who
deposed the Mother. Grigg's conclusion is that if
Pearson "can find a receptive audience in Utah
. . . she can make it anywhere."[60]

The Sexual Revolution. This radical ideological
feminism is, in some sense, an inevitable reaction to
and extension of the sexual revolution of the sixties.
Unleashed in a culture traditionally patterned on
Judeo-Christian ethics, this "liberalization" at first
catered to heterosexual male appetites and produced the image of the woman as sexual object. In
its own way, this heterosexual revolution was an assault against the image of God in men and women.
But now the pendulum has swung in the other direction. Feminism is demanding revenge. Such a
movement gets rid of certain expressions of unjus-
tifiable male oppression, but its real ideological goal
is to efface any recollection of creational structures.
It is surprising that a non-Christian (at least he lays
no claim to being a Christian in his books), once
feminist thinker, George Gilder, has (since 1973)
recognized this ideological agenda whereas the
thinking of so many Christians appears naively
oblivious. Gilder notes:

> The revolutionary members of the women's move-
> ment . . . say that our sexual relationships are fun-

62

damental to all our other institutions and activities. If one could profoundly change the relations between the sexes, they contend, one could radically and unrecognizably transform the society.[61]

Gilder rightly affirms that "sexuality is not simply a matter of *Games People Play;* it is one of the few matters truly of life and death to society."[62] Thus he warns that if the feminist agenda, even its more moderate version,[63] is carried through, "our society is doomed to years of demoralization and anarchy, possibly ending in a police state."[64] It would be easy to dismiss Gilder as an extremist, but one only has to read in the New Age literature to see that police states are definitely on the final agenda. One must seriously ask, therefore, to what extent the present evangelical landslide capitulation to various forms of contemporary feminism is the result of new Spirit-inspired insight into the deep meaning of Scripture.[65] Is it not rather the unwitting adoption and imposition upon Scripture of an alien ideology bent upon the annihilation of orthodox Christianity? Certainly we should do all we can to hear Scripture afresh as it pertains to the role and ministry of Christian women. But the specter of the destruction of our God-given sexually differentiated identities in the name of Christ should fill us with righteous loathing and dread.[66]

Democracy: One More God to Worship in the New Age Pantheon. Brilliantly packaged as a self-evident truth of the sacred democratic process, the Aquarian agenda of gay rights, abortion rights, and feminism has managed to make enormous strides in gaining acceptance in mainstream America.[67] Sexual equality as a self-evident political right then becomes a self-evident ecclesiastical right. This is the argument of evangelical scholar Patricia Gundry.

> When I researched my first book, I discovered a process at work in the movement of democracy towards equalizing opportunity for all people in this country. I noticed the confluence of that democratic progress with other forces to produce issues that would come alive and stay alive until changes were made. One such issue is the contemporary issue of equality for women. It is especially interesting to see the confluence of influences at work in the case of the equality for women in the Church. . . . You could probably blame [Christian women's insistence on equality within the church] on democracy and be at least partly right. Women are only behaving as though they believe in democracy and live in a democratic country. In a democratic society issues continually bubble into public awareness for measuring against the democratic ideal. If you look backward at the history of this country, you can see the upward percolation of issue after issue, measuring practice against the democratic ideal. . . . Slavery was one such issue, voting rights another. . . . At this time the issue of women's reality and the conflict between that reality and the democratic ideal is in the public arena.[68]

Ironically, the same democratic system that declares God politically and ethically nonexistent somehow functions by divine right and necessity in promoting the cause of Christian liberty. The secular, democratic state has succeeded in removing from the public domain the two essential elements that define our humanity—God and gender distinctions. As a case in point, in the over one hundred textbooks used in the state-school system in 1985, not one single story or theme celebrated motherhood, while sex role reversals were common.[69] How is it that the most indispensable sexual role for the maintenance of civilization is "carefully and systematically expunged from the official cultural record?"[70] One wonders how "democracy," which itself demands a strict separation between church and state, and at the same time is hell-bent on promoting the modern sexual ideology of androgyny, can be so uncritically adopted as a major factor in the elaboration of Christian ethics and ecclesiology. Are all causes adopted as expressions of the democratic ideal to be espoused by the Christian faith?

Take homosexuality. "You can't stop the music," taunts the gay music group Village People. Indeed, who would dare? The knees of most politicians turn to jelly when gays demand minority status as a civil rights movement. But before homosexuality is included among self-evident truths by the emotive deployment of democratic buzz words, it might be good for us to stop and ask just *who* is *writing* the music? Are we composing the next verse of the hymn to human freedom, or are malefic powers, bent on the destruction of humanity, now calling the tune?

Meanwhile the civil rights march gayly rolls on. Says one leading lesbian, "The biggest issue is making homosexuality as normal as heterosexuality."[71] The project is clearly succeeding in modern-day America, in spite of the scores of millions of Americans who doubtless oppose it. The case of Bill McCartney, winning football coach at the University of Colorado in Boulder, is indicative of the vocal and political power of the supporters of homosexuality. As an evangelical Christian McCartney feels obliged to speak out against homosexuality and abortion, but his civic and spiritual rights are being denied him by a vociferous group on campus. "This university must keep this man in line. He has demonstrated time and time again that he needs to be kept on a leash. He is using his position to create an atmosphere of hate and fear on this campus," says a leading senior student. Regents and faculty members accuse him of "hate-mongering" and call him "a self-anointed ayatollah." The student union government is "absolutely disgusted" by his expressed beliefs, and many are calling for his ouster. McCartney is not planning to back down, though. "I may be just a football coach," he says, "but I'm not going to stand aside on the tough issues facing society."

The double-standard being applied in cases like this defies belief. The gay rights people jump on any occasion to promote homosexuality whenever they can find well-known personalities willing to defend

them. There are no calls for ouster. Many presti-
gious news media are using their enormous powers
to promote homosexuality in millions of homes
across America. Why deny Bill McCartney the freedom to express his views?[72]

Time Magazine invites its readers to accept
homosexuality the way they accepted African
Americans, women voters, or automated-teller ma-
chines. According to staff contributor, Andrew
Tobias: "Most people are straight, some people are
gay, and it's really not that big a deal. Sometimes
it's even funny." No doubt Tobias will be amused
when Hot and Hunky Hamburger of San
Francisco starts franchises on Main Streets all over
America. *Time* asks its readers to accept homosexuality for patriotic reasons. "In the long run [this
will] make America stronger and more competi-
tive."[73] Yes, perhaps, in the hamburger trade, but
sexual perversion is notorious for bringing down
civilizations.

The point of the *Time* article is that homosexuality is here to stay because it has been accepted
in that bastion of right-wing conservatism, the
Harvard Business School. Indeed in a further article, on bisexuality, *Time* completes the normaliza-
tion of sodomy in full conformity to the strategy of
gay and lesbian pressure groups. Its readers are
asked to consider the possibility that heterosexual
and homosexual alternatives are really normal when
compared to bisexuality, which is a sign of unnat-
ural sexual confusion or repression.[74]

In other words, gays are straight. And the beat

goes on. In its recent annual meeting the governing body of the American Bar Association went two significant notches to the left. It opposed all federal and state restrictions on abortion and voted to affiliate the National Lesbian and Gay Law Association.[75] If venerable institutions such as *Time* and Harvard Business School, with their enormous powers of influence, as well as the majority of lawyers, have been won over to the homosexual cause (not to speak of abortion), it is perhaps not too outlandish to think that the moral, Christian majority has just lost America.

In the name of democracy contemporary society accepts and sanctions homosexuality, but should the church sanction practicing homosexuals and admit them to the Christian ministry? Unthinkably, some now do, causing one to wonder if the process will ever stop. The North American Man-Boy Love Association (NAMBLA), an organized pedophile group, employs the same rationale, arguing that laws forbidding consensual sex between adults and children are symptoms of an oppressive society afflicted with sexual hang-ups. A spokesman of the group boldly states: "We see ourselves as a civil rights group. . . . we see our platform as the liberation of young people."[76] As homosexuality is legally institutionalized and more and more accepted as a normal expression of human sexuality, pedophilia will likely become a major civil rights issue. The proof? Pedophilia was deemed the most noble form of sexuality in ancient Greece, the culture that gave us democracy.[77]

Clearly democracy and the biblical definition of sexuality do not always agree! Unfortunately some orthodox Christians, under the societal pressure of the democratic process, which they often identify as "the Spirit of God," seem ready to accept the democratic agenda even if that means flying in the face of clear scriptural teaching on the structures of creation. F. Sontag, writing in the British *Evangelical Quarterly*,[78] notes:

> Lesbian and homosexual tolerance are often included on the feminist's agenda [through which the Spirit has doubtless appeared[79]] for the release from prejudice. True, God cannot be seen as utterly opposed to this, since . . . the biological scheme divinity[80] decided upon allows multiple roles between the sexes. However, since reproduction is largely . . . limited to heterosexuality, it is hard to see homosexuality as God's first choice.

Of course, since the biological scheme "allows" pedophilia, even bestiality, could we not eventually allow these as "divinity's" third and fourth choices? You've come a long way, baby! But this is playing with fire, and everyone is going to get burned!

Here in the powerful domain of sexual identity it would clearly seem that the Gnostic empire is striking back with a vengeance. This New Age attack is more widespread and profound than most imagine.[81] Exploiting modern sensitivity to the theme of democratic justice, it reaches to the very core of what it means to be a man or a woman created in the image of God.

TECHNIQUES FOR SELF-KNOWLEDGE: GOING WITHIN VIA A PASSAGE TO INDIA

The current fascination among many in the unsuspecting general public for yoga techniques to aid in exercise and relaxation is not merely an interesting but unimportant footnote of contemporary social history. Rather it is one more indication of the infiltration of the New Age world view into Western life. Just like ancient pagan Gnosticism, New Age self-consciousness needs stimulation by what Shirley MacLaine calls "spiritual technology." As part of her meditation, she does "a silent mantra [Hindu chant] with each of my hatha yoga poses. I hold each yoga position for twenty seconds and internally chant, 'I am God in light.'"[82] In the same way, unsuspecting yuppies in yoga-inspired exercise classes in suburbia everywhere chant the Hindu "om" ("aaauuuummmm"), "I am." MacLaine goes on to explain the use of crystals and the Hindu chakras—points of different colored light within the body that represent the seven aspects of spiritual energy and self-consciousness making up the higher self. Others speak of Ouija boards, levitation, out of body experiences, and astral projection. Finally occult channeling and possession lift one into this higher realm of existence, often, alas, with chilling consequences.[83] The adoption of Hindu meditative techniques is widespread in New Age spiritual technology. Thus the warning from Suresh Chander Verma, a converted Hindu priest, should be taken with extreme seriousness. He notes that the goal of meditation is self-realization through self-knowledge. These techniques give a sense of indestructibility as one's spirit becomes independent of one's decaying body and is identified with the universal divine. It is the old lie of the Devil—"You will become like God." Since, Verma argues, no one can be like God, such a procedure leads inevitably to the loss of any true identity and even to self-destruction, Satan's ultimate goal.[84]

DRAWING THE GNOSTIC-NEW AGE COMPARISON: A LOOK AT THE BOTTOM LINE

If you are responsible for the family budget or for balancing the company's books, you know the importance of the bottom line. The comparison I have proposed here is historically fascinating for those who like history, and theologically instructive for amateur theologians. But these elements are not the bottom line.

I have underscored the most striking elements of comparison between the two systems. In its planetary vision and one-world philosophy, the New Age has gone far beyond Gnosticism. Mark Satin's vision of the New Age society that is "androgynous and feminist, neo-occult and paganistic, tribal and co-operative . . . and globally planetized"[85] is much more extensive and programmatic than anything the Gnostics wrote. Nevertheless the lines of agreement in basic structure are profound, as the layers of Christendom are pulled away after a silence of 1500 years, so as to justify thinking that the same Gnostic empire is striking back, but now with renewed and added force.

THE GNOSTIC EMPIRE IS STRIKING BACK

This is the bottom line. History, albeit diabolical history, is repeating itself before our very eyes. We can therefore begin to understand the changes taking place in our contemporary culture. The Earth Summit, homosexuality, feminism, mandated cultural and ethnic diversity, etc., are not unrelated phenomena associated with the chaotic transmutation of our modern, unstable society. As various hues of the same rainbow,[86] they are all deeply related aspects of a coherent religious agenda whose goal is the creation of a new humanity made in the image of the god of this world. This bottom line should convince you to take the New Age Movement with utmost seriousness. Every Christian should be involved in understanding the nature of this redoubtable adversary, in order both to avoid being trapped by one or more of the programs on offer, and to rethink one's own faith and witness in the light of this pernicious heresy.

NOTES

1. 62.34ff.
2. Even some orthodox Christian scholars have now

dropped the distinctively Christian way of dividing history. B.C. and A.D. are giving way to B.C.E. (before common era) and C.E. (common era). At this level, too, the Age of Pisces is on the wane!

3. Recounted by Richard Winter, "From Pisces to Aquarius: Overtaken by the New Age," L'Abri Tapes.

4. Ibid.

5. Mariam Starhawk, *The Spiritual Dance: A Rebirth of the Ancient Religion of the Great Goddess* (New York: Harper and Row, 1979), 9.

6. Dawne McCance, "Understandings of 'The Goddess' in Contemporary Feminism," in Larry W. Hurtado, ed., *Goddesses in Religions and Modern Debate: University of Manitoba Studies in Religion* (Atlanta, Ga.: Scholars Press, 1990)1:169.

7. Shirley MacLaine, *Going Within: A Guide for Inner Transformation* (New York: Bantam Books, 1989), 204-5, 210.

8. Ibid., 136.

9. Mark Satin, in his book, *New Age Politics: The Healing Self and Society* (New York: Dell Books, 1978), 20-23, calls the mind-set of this present age a six-sided prison, recalling the Gnostic denigration of the body as the prison-house of the soul. It would be interesting to know to what extent reincarnation is related to the Gnostic notion of the soul's journey back to ultimate being, being obliged to penetrate through 365 aeons or spheres with the correct password in order to arrive at the highest plane. The Hindu expects countless reincarnations before realizing union with God (see Suresh Chander Verma, *Satanic Foundations of Hinduism and Yoga* [Kansas City, Mo.: (self-published), 1983], 16).

10. Tal Brooke, *Lord of the Air: Tales of a Modern AntiChrist* (Eugene, Oreg.: Harvest House, 1990), 68. Verma, as an ex-guru, speaks of the lie of the Devil, who promises as the prize for meditation that one will be like God. It is a lie because no one is like God, so that the end result is "losing everything you have, your existence and everything" (ibid.).

11. MacLaine, *Going Within*, 210-11.

12. C. S. Lewis, *The Silver Chair* (New York: Collier Books, 1953, 1970), 159-60.

13. Winter, "From Pisces to Aquarius."

14. Karen L. King, "Ridicule and Rape, Rule and Rebellion," in J. E. Goehring, *Gnosticism and the Early Christian World* (Sonoma, Calif.: Polebridge Press, 1990), 23-24.

15. Rita Gross, "Hindu Female Deities as a Resource for the Contemporary Discovery of the Goddess," in Carl Olson, ed., *The Book of the Goddess: Past and Present* (New York: Crossroads, 1983), 217-18, cited in McCance, "'The Goddess' in Contemporary Feminism," 174.

16. See Klaus K. Klostermaier, "Sakti: Hindu Images and Concepts of the Goddess," in Hurtado, ed., *Goddesses in Religions*, 149.

17. Joan B. Townsend, "The Goddess: Fact, Fallacy and Revitalization Movement," *Goddesses in Religions*, 179ff.

18. Ibid., 181.

19. Cited in Brooke, *When the World*, 175.

20. See the back cover.

21. Interestingly, the goddess in Hindu Saktism wears a snake as a pendant, and, in another representation, her breast is bound with a serpent. See Klostermaier, "Sakti," in Hurtado, ed., *Goddesses in Religions*, 147, 152, who also notes that sexual promiscuity, black magic, and sorcery often accompanied this goddess spirituality.

22. This would appear to be an excellent example of the elasticity permitted by the feminist "hermeneutic of suspicion," which enables the text of the Bible to be "unraveled" and then put back together again according to one's own philosophy.

23. Primavesi, *From Apocalypse to Genesis*, 233, emphasis mine.

24. Ibid., 234-35, emphasis mine.

25. (Minneapolis: Fortress, 1991), 143.

26. Francis Watson, "Strategies of Recovery and Resistance: Hermeneutical Reflections on Genesis 1-3 and Its Pauline Reception," *Journal for the Study of the New Testament*

45 (March 1992): 79-103, emphasis added. Watson teaches in the department of theology and religious studies, King's College, London.

27. Cited in Richard Smith, "Afterword: the Modern Relevance of Gnosticism," The Nag Hammadi Library in English, trans. members of the Coptic Gnostic Library Project of the Institute for Antiquity and Christianity, James M. Robinson, Director (San Francisco: Harper and Row, 1988), 548.

28. See also the work of Harold Bloom, *The Book of J* (New York: Grove Wiedenfeld, 1990) who argues that the hypothetical source "J" of the Pentateuch was written by an unbelieving woman of the tenth century B.C. This unknown female author presents Jahweh as a bungler and favors the serpent. Bruce Waltke's estimation of J as "the most blasphemous writer that ever lived" was written before the appearance of Primavesi's work, and makes no mention of the Gnostics. See B. Waltke, "Harold Bloom and 'J': A Review Article," *Journal of the Evangelical Theological Society* (December 1991): 509.

29. Brooke, *When the World*, 210.

30. See Douglas R. Groothuis, *Unmasking the New Age* (Downers Grove, Ill.: InterVarsity, 1986), 154.

31. Interestingly, in Hinduism, meditation on the self is associated with the serpent. According to Tal Brooke, *Lord of the Air*, 143, he was taught by the great guru Sai Baba that the goal of meditation was enlightenment. "When this happened the secret sushumna passage would open within the spinal cord sending the ancient Kundalini Serpent power through the seven chakra power centers along the spine as one became enlightened; here was the mysterious secret of the ancient Sekurati tree, the tree of wisdom in the Kabbala." Brooke describes (186) the time he was allowed into the private apartment of Sai Baba, where few were ever admitted, and being overwhelmed by the fact that the bed, in the form of a lotus flower, had a wooden canopy carved into the shape of the ancient serpent Seshma. (Brooke also notes

that the serpent was a symbol in Wicca and Druid spirituality.)

32. Carol Christ, "Why Women Need the Goddess: Phenomenological, Psychological and Political Reflections," in Christ and Plaskow, *Womanspirit Rising: A Feminist Reader in Religion* (San Francisco: Harper and Row, 1979), 277.

33. MacLaine, *Going Within*, 56-57.

34. Ibid., 75, 79.

35. Cited by Hippolytus, *Refutation of All Heresies* 8:15:1-2. See Elaine Pagels, *The Gnostic Gospels* (New York: Random House, 1981), xix.

36. *Christian Systematic Theology* (Minneapolis: Augsburg Fortress, 1991), 441, emphasis mine. This sounds suspiciously like New Age meditation techniques for going within.

37. According to Douglas R. Groothuis, *Revealing the New Age Jesus* (Downers Grove, Ill.: InterVarsity, 1990), 20.

38. Quoted in Brooke, *When the World*, 127.

39. Cited in Groothuis, *Revealing the New Age Jesus*, 196.

40. Cited in Douglas R. Groothuis, "The Shamanized Jesus," *Christianity Today*, April 29, 1991, 20.

41. Ibid.

42. Page 14, cited in Constance Cumbey, *The Hidden Dangers of the Rainbow* (Lafayette, La.: Huntington House, 1983), 31-32.

43. See chapter 3, under the heading, "Christology: Christ Our Twin Brother."

44. Cited in Groothuis, "The Shamanized Jesus," 20.

45. Primavesi, *From Apocalypse*, 237. Primavesi turns this into a good, for it identifies Jesus with the world.

46. MacLaine, *Going Within*, 218. This rejection of Christianity's particularism in favor of syncretism recalls the remark of Arnold Toynbee that the mark of a culture's last stage is not decay but syncretism. See *Reconsiderations* (New York: Oxford University Press, 1961), 446, cited in H. Schlossberg, *Idols for Destruction* (New York: Thomas Nelson, 1983), 269.

47. Texe Marrs, *Dark Secrets of the New Age*

(Westchester, Ill.: Crossway, 1987), 123.

48. Quoted in ibid., 123.

49. *Against Heresies,* Preface, 2.

50. Brooke, *When the World,* 68.

51. MacLaine, *Going Within,* 100.

52. Winter, "From Pisces to Aquarius."

53. MacLaine, *Going Within,* 87.

54. Ibid., 96, 189.

55. Ibid., 196-97

56. McCance, "'The Goddess' in Contemporary Feminism," 168, characterizing the works of Letty Russell, Phyllis Trible, and Rita Gross.

57. Giovanni Filoramo, *A History of Gnosticism,* trans. Anthony Alcock (Oxford: Basil Blackwell, 1990), 61.

58. Published in 1992.

59. See Brooke, *When the World,* 210.

60. William Grigg in *Chronicles,* March 1992, 6.

61. George Gilder, *Sexual Suicide* (New York: New York Times, 1973), 192. This book was revised in 1986 under the title, *Men and Marriage* (Gretna: Pellican).

62. Ibid., 80.

63. The moderates of the women's movement "want legislation and power that will apply to everyone and change the very nature of society. They want to establish the professional woman with secondary family affiliation . . . as the American norm." This goal undermines "the most important source of stability in civilized society—the female role in the family" (ibid., 152). It is the moderate demand for equality in the work-force (compare the same demand *mutatis mutandis* in the church "work-force") that produces a situation "never before undergone by males anywhere in the world, except perhaps in a few decaying tribes and in the ghetto. . . . [namely] the prospect of the collective and systematic entrance of millions of women . . . professing a determination to compete in remorseless equality, and calling on the intervention of government to assure their rights. . . . We thus have an all-out attack on the male role as provider and on the masculine ritu-

als of work. We have a prescription for social paralysis and a concerted lapse of male socialization unprecedented in a civilized society" (186).

64. Ibid., 112.

65. Patricia Gundry claims that a new, more sophisticated science of hermeneutics makes feminist biblical interpretation possible (*Neither Slave Nor Free* [New York: Harper and Row, 1987], 77-78). Elizabeth Schlussler Fiorenza, "Changing the Paradigms," in *How My Mind Has Changed,* ed. James M. Wall and David Heim (Grand Rapids: Eerdmans, 1991), 86, proposes a "hermeneutic of suspicion," capable of unraveling "the patriarchal politics inscribed in the biblical text. Since the Bible is written in androcentric, grammatically masculine language that can function as generic inclusive or as patriarchal exclusive language, feminist interpretation must develop a 'hermeneutic of critical evaluation for proclamation' that is able to assess theologically whether scriptural texts function to inculcate patriarchal values [the reader is left to imagine what she would do with those], or whether they must be read against their linguistic 'androcentric grain' in order to set free their liberating vision for today and for the future. Such a feminist hermeneutics of liberation reconceptualizes the understanding of Scripture as nourishing bread rather than as unchanging sacred word engraved in stone."

Gilder's simple and profound observations of the way males and females differ and complement one another, without any Christian pretense, does far greater justice to Scripture than this so-called biblical feminist hermeneutic.

66. While no doubt seeking to avoid groundless stereotypes, Patricia Gundry's desire to avoid what she considers a sexist up-bringing for her children, surely, in view of the New Age ideology of sex, may run perilously close to adopting their androgynous model (*Neither Slave Nor Free* [New York: Harper and Row, 1987], 45).

67. Gilder, *Sexual Suicide,* 135, shows how the demand for abortion is not simply the alleviation of economic or psychological hardship. "It is part of a movement that is chang-

ing the sexual dimensions of every human relationship and every exchange of love. . . . the reluctance of the people to authorize abortion on demand stems from a profound sense of justifiable conservatism in interfering with our deepest human experiences." In 1972 80 percent of the voters in North Dakota voted against liberalized abortion laws. Already in the space of twenty years this has changed dramatically.

68. Gundry, *Neither Slave Nor Free*, 4, 76-77.

69. Paul C. Vitz, "A Study of Religion and Traditional Values in Public School Textbooks," a paper presented at the conference, "Democracy and the Renewal of Public Education," (New York, N.Y., 1985, cited in Maggie Gallagher, *Enemies of Eros* (Chicago: Bonus Books, 1989), 8. Vitz is professor of psychology at New York University. Maggie Gallagher is a single mother.

70. Gallagher, *Enemies of Eros*, 9

71. See the *Los Angeles Times*, March 15, 1992, 43.

72. See the *Los Angeles Times*, March 25, 1992, C3.

73. *Time*, March 23, 1992, 47. Tobias is a respected staff contributor, mentioned alongside Charles Krauthammer, Stephan Kanfer, Richard Schickel, R. Z. Sheppard, Jay Cocks, et al.

74. *Time*, August 17, 1992, 50. Needless to say, the bisexuals are organized and politically active. Their civil-sexual rights must also be protected, for they cannot go on "racked by discomfort and conflict" (51).

75. *Los Angeles Times*, August 12, 1992.

76. See *Los Angeles Times*, March 11, 1992.

77. See the highly scholarly work of K. J. Dover, *Greek Homosexuality* (Cambridge, Mass.: Harvard University Press, 1978), who notes, 121-22, "The quantity of materials [inscriptions, pottery, etc.] is evidence of the male society's preoccupation with the beauty of boys and youths. . . . the characteristic Greek conception of sexuality [is] a relationship between a senior and a junior [male] partner." Plato and, no doubt, Socrates were pedophiles (153-54). Even Zeus, the highest god, was considered a pedophile (119). A widely found

terracotta statuette shows Zeus carrying of the boy Ganymede, who appears to be around ten or twelve years old.

78. F. Sontag, "Barth, Romans and Feminist Theology," *Evangelical Quarterly* 63 (October 1991): 321.

79. Ibid., 329.

80. This is Sontag's awkward way of avoiding the masculine gender for God. The unfortunate result is that God loses an essential element of personality.

81. Few Christian writers on the New Age seem to be aware of the enormous influence of "Gnostic" thinking on the contemporary view of sexuality—or are politically not willing to denounce it.

82. MacLaine, *Going Within,* 68.

83. See Tal Brooke, *When the World,* 54. Brooks Alexander remarks that the "various systems of 'enlightenment' and occult mysticism train people to be agents of their own dissolution" ("Breathing Together: Conspiracy and Intention," *S.C.P. Journal* 16, 2 [1991]: 6).

Verma's comparison between Hinduism and New Age thinking is interesting (see his *Satanic Foundations,* 16, 27) inasmuch as scholars are beginning to trace the roots of ancient Gnosticism in Hinduism. See Hermann Kloss, *Gnostizismus und "Erkenntnispfad"* (Leiden: Brill, 1983), and Pagels, *Adam, Eve and the Serpent,* 65. Alexander the Great's Hellenic empire extended to India and affected Hindu statuary. No doubt influences also went in the other direction.

84. Verma, *Satanic Foundations,* 16, 27.

85. Satin, *New Age Politics,* cited in Brooke, *When the World,* 208.

86. Constance Cumbey writes, in the foreword to *Hidden Dangers:* "The New Age Movement uses rainbows to signify their building of the Rainbow Bridge (antahkarana) between man and Lucifer who, they say, is the over-soul. New Agers place small rainbow decals on their automobiles and book stores as a signal to others in the Movement."

5

Perspectives for the Planet and for the Church

What are the immediate perspectives for this new-look spirituality as we approach the formidable year 2000? What does this *fin de siecle,* the end of the second millennium, hold out for the world and for the Christian church? Should the church be concerned by the reappearance of Christianized paganism? Will the New Age peter out like so many other strange cults from Southern California? Or does the future look bright for this revamped form of ancient Gnosticism?

THE NEW GNOSTICISM IS HERE TO STAY

The New Age is the "fastest growing alternate belief system in the country."

So said Christian apologist, Norman Geisler in his book, *Apologetics in the New Age.*[1] Such remarkable growth is not happening by chance. New Age guru Marilyn Ferguson pointedly entitles her book *The Aquarian Conspiracy* and announces, "Power-filled, self-realized individuals stand poised to enact 'a benign conspiracy for a new human agenda' on a large scale."[2] "'Aquarian Conspiracy' is the term I have coined," she says, "for the network of people working for social transformation based on personal inner change. . . . These people, who are advocates of what I call the Aquarian Conspiracy paradigm shift are formidable."[3] Recently Ferguson has called the New Age Movement "the third largest religious denomination in America."[4] Its adepts are formidable because they are highly motivated and well educated.[5] They are trading their wares in mainline America. Over a hundred Fortune 500 companies use New Age seminars to put their personnel in touch with the deep spiritual force within them, for many of the hippies of the sixties and seventies have now become corporate yuppies. Recently, the *Los Angeles Times* ran an article on Jerry Rubin. Remember in 1968 the bare-chested, long-haired Rubin, member of the Chicago Seven who screamed, "Capitalism killed my father"? This same Jerry Rubin in 1992 is a successful capitalistic businessman, selling, incidentally, strange pseudo-drugs/nutrients for the brain, convinced that freedom is still number one on his agenda.[6] The use of LSD, the chemical short-cut to self-knowledge, otherwise known in Hinduism as the experience of *Nirvikalpa samadhi* or the highest mystical state,[7] is again on the rise

among American teenagers.[8] Yogic exercises are re-
placing aerobics among the in-crowd yuppies. "I
leave feeling like I am on drugs," says one. Others
describe the experience as "spiritual elevation."[9]
The progress of New Age ideology in the public
educational system, at the United Nations, in the
military, and in churches is well documented.[10]

EVEN TOLERANCE HAS ITS LIMITS— "CURLING AROUND" THE FANATICS!

The New Age spirituality is selling like free
Super Bowl tickets. In the world and the church
more and more people are finding irresistible its ideology of common survival for a threatened humanity and a polluted planet.[11] Our endangered "global
village" is seeking global solutions,[12] not just ecological but spiritual.[13] As the demon of atheistic
Marxism is being cast out, seven more are rushing
in, taking the form of a one-world humanistic spirituality. In its all-embracing tolerance, only one
form of spirituality will ultimately not be tolerated—
biblical Christianity. Inconceivably, traditional faith
is more and more accused of being the source and
perhaps one day will be branded the scapegoat of
humanity's present ills. The new brand of pluralistic, planetary Christianity as expressed by Smart
and Konstantine will take care of Christian orthodoxy. These authors identify not only with the
World Council of Churches but also with the World
Congress of Faiths, an organism seeking to join all
religions. Their noble desire is to promote friend-

ship and cooperation in order to "overcome fanaticism in the world, because it is dangerous and often expresses groupist hatred." They go on:

> But we shall not overcome it [fanaticism] by frontal assault, by being fanatically anti-fanatical. . . . we must remember Gandhi and other saints. . . . It may be that through ecumenical banding together of like-minded religionists we may curl around the fanatics, so that at least the next generation and maybe they themselves will learn to love a softer Light.[14]

Perhaps a harbinger of things to come, there are two stories treated in very different ways in the same issue of the *Los Angeles Times*, on February 5, 1992. One concerns the allegations brought against the Los Angeles Assistant Police Chief, Robert L. Vernon, accused of being a "fundamentalist" Christian on the job, allegedly guilty, among other things, of doodling Christian fish signs on official memos. In an editorial cartoon, God is reaching down (as in Michelangelo's "The Creation of Adam") with the message, "Vernon for L.A.P.D. Chief." The cartoon is clearly intended to block the realization of this "divine plan." And the cartoon worked. Two weeks later, in a story on the finalists for the post of chief of the Los Angeles Police Department, there is the terse statement: "Assistant Chief Robert L. Vernon, who has been accused of improperly infusing his fundamentalist religious views into his police work, was eliminated from the competition." The only accompanying comment is the report that the present chief Darryl Gates is "distressed" that good candidates such as Vernon have been eliminated.[15]

The other story is an enthusiastic account of a New Age boarding school for youths between the ages of thirteen and twenty-five, the Nizhoni School for Global Consciousness, in Santa Fe, New Mexico. Among other things, the school teaches planet management and spirituality ("not religion"!)—i.e., self-discovery through the awareness of previous lives—and that all people are part of the universal higher self. These things are taught "all with the blessings of the state education officials," notes the *Times* reporter. Indeed the state board gave the school accreditation even though neither the founder, Chris Griscom, one of Shirley MacLaine's gurus, nor the president, Alex Petofi, had a teaching certificate.[16] Without so much as a question about the impingement of religion on state education, the article ends with the hope of Griscom that this unconventional alternate education "will one day be adopted by mainstream educators."

As one author has noted, the politically correct intelligentsia has already "judged the gospel of Christ to be 'sexist, racist, anti-semitic, patriarchal, chauvinistic and homophobic'"[17] and is opting more and more for the New Age creed of globalism, which denies sin, idealizes human potential, and is so profoundly politically correct.

Tal Brooke rightly sees that a "New World Order has no patience with any non-inclusive belief system."[18] Brooke asks the question concerning the fate of religious freedom in a unified world. He puts it graphically and perhaps not unrealistically, basing his projection on the present United Nations resolution concerning religious tolerance.

> Any exclusive faith or belief claiming unique revelation would be a supreme offense to the "unity in diversity" mandate for public peace. The newly curtailed and docile Christians would look no different outwardly than the rest. . . . Evangelists could be arrested for committing "crimes against the people," while Christians could be dismissed for "hate crimes" if they shared their faith with anyone.

Already this is becoming a reality on some campuses. Of the situation on the Stanford campus, Tim Stafford, explains, "The university, in trying to stamp out intolerance, has created an atmosphere in which people believe they have 'a right not to be offended.'" One student recounts that "it's fine to admit that I'm a Christian. . . . it's cool that I am into spirituality. But if I were to try to 'impose my views,' then I've gone over my limits." The author goes on to observe, "Christians are tolerated but at a price: they keep a 'silent contract.'" Thus Christian students "admit that most of the time they keep controversial thoughts (about abortion, homosexuality, etc.) to themselves."[19] This is the other side of the same reality about which Brooke speaks in his analysis of the United Nations resolution on religious freedom. Brooke tries to imagine what society would be like if the resolution were put into effect.

"To put it in Orwellian terms . . . people would be free not to share their faith; they would be free not to judge anything morally or otherwise critique any spiritual beliefs . . . in the interest of the pluralistic majority, they would be absolutely compelled to live as though their faith were nothing more than a highly privatized prejudice."[20] What Brooke in 1991 extrapolates from the United Nations resolution is actually going on at Stanford in 1992. One has to wonder if Rev. Jerry Falwell was aware of these forces when he recently gave such optimistic appraisal of the health of the Religious Right. "I do not think a new thrust is needed. Our evangelical public out there no longer needs a general. They know where they are. . . . We're in place now."[21] While it is true that our place in heaven is secure, there is no promise in Scripture that the church can count on any places down here. Certainly the New Age Movement's reach for global power should give Christians food for thought concerning secure places in this present world.

THE NEW GNOSTICISM'S NEW-LOOK CANON: A REVISED THEORETICAL BASIS FOR NEW AGE CHRISTIANITY

Something strange is happening. At a time when ancient Gnosticism is returning in the brand new clothes of New Age spirituality, some circles of contemporary New Testament scholarship are seeking to reclaim the ancient Gnostic texts as authentic *Christian* literature. While on the popular level, occult channelers and long-haired gurus of all hues promote magical mystery tours of the inner self, highly respected academicians in conservative suits and ivy-covered buildings defend Gnosticism as a legitimate variant expression of early Christianity. There seems no possible relationship. These phenomena are worlds apart. Each of the two groups would probably have difficulty admitting the other's spiritual validity. And yet the troublesome enigma will not go away. If the thesis of this book is correct, there is a common source that, through vastly different methods and procedures, appears to be leading to the same ultimate goal.

TIED GAME: QUMRAN 1—NAG HAMMADI 1

At the end of the forties, a great scholarly card game played itself out. In 1948, those favoring a Jewish Old Testament background of the New Testament slammed down on the table of New Testament studies a seemingly unbeatable ace, the discovery of the Qumran documents. These ancient, pre-Christian texts demonstrated for the first time that so many ideas considered of pagan Greek origin were in fact perfectly Jewish. But then critical liberalism countered with an ace of its own, that of the discovery in the same year of the Nag Hammadi texts. Some Egyptian peasants had unearthed a library of the most ancient Gnostic documents ever discovered. While the case for Jewish and Old Testament backgrounds has been fundamentally strengthened, the Gnostic empire is striking back in the hallowed halls of New Testament science, thanks to the Nag Hammadi Gnostic library. Some perhaps hope that this will constitute a knockout punch for orthodox Christianity, especially since the Egyptian peasant who found the texts, having smashed the large jar that contained them, bore the appropriate name of Mohammed Ali.

Under the assault of ideological feminism, many are becoming dissatisfied with the church's canon. For example, Susan Durber, a feminist New Testament scholar, can no longer read Jesus' parables recorded in Luke 15. For her, they were written by men for men. Since these texts are "impossible" to read, "we will need to write new ones," she declares, "but that of course, will have problems of its own."[22] Rosemary Radford Ruether, the well-known spokeswoman of feminist theology, does not hesitate to express the radical conclusions to which her thinking leads her.

> Feminist theology must create a new textual base, a new canon. . . . Feminist theology cannot be done from the existing base of the Christian Bible.[23]

Have they not realized? The problem is solved! Feminist spirituality will not be obliged to write new texts. The canon for which they long *has* been available for some forty years. The Gnostic documents of Nag Hammadi will more than adequately fill the bill. Finally humanistic Christianity will have its own canon, hoary with age and capable of making a claim to authenticity.

Being obliged to work with other people's Scripture, liberalism's freedom of action has been thus limited. But now it has ancient texts to support its redefinition of Christianity. This will no doubt be a knock-out punch for many naive believers! One commentator has said that Elaine Pagels's book *The Gnostic Gospels* "did more than any other . . . to ingratiate the Gnostics to modern Americans. She made them accessible, even likeable."[24] Pagels made them likeable because she obviously espouses many of their cherished beliefs. If modern Americans like ancient Gnostics, how could they possibly resist contemporary New Agers?

JESUS, VERY GODDESS—A NEW LEASE ON LIFE

A whole wing of New Testament studies is committed to a clearly defined revolutionary program, namely the "Dismantling and Reassembling of the Categories of New Testament Scholarship." Such is the title of an article by James Robinson, director of the Institute for Antiquity and Christianity and the Coptic Gnostic Library Project, and recent president of the Society of Biblical Literature.[25] Translated from elegant scholarly jargon, this means the rehabilitation in today's church of the ancient Gnostic heresy. In barely veiled terms, ancient Gnosticism and its modern equivalent—"the counter-culture movements coming from the 60's"—are presented as the exciting religious challenge to today's tired society.[26] For

Robinson, this is theological motivation for the study of the Nag Hammadi library. For Robinson and others in his school, Gnosticism and orthodoxy are proposed as two possible but relative ways—"trajectories"—of interpreting early Christianity. Indeed heresy just as reasonably as orthodoxy may trace its roots back into the New Testament. Heresy and orthodoxy are no longer meaningful terms. According to the pluralistic vision of left-wing scholarship (it may even be called mainstream science by now) these are merely various equally valid theological options that the winners of the struggle, orthodox churchmen, decided to brand in such a polemical way. Robinson traces early Gnostic thinking back to the Corinthians and to "Q,"[27] the hypothetical document supposedly embedded in the canonical Gospels Matthew and Luke. Robinson considers Q, along with the *Gospel of Thomas,* among the earliest collections of Jesus sayings.[28] Since, like Thomas, Q has no interest in the death and resurrection of Jesus, it is clear that "Jesus rose, [not at a point in time but] as the revalidation of his word, into the [always present] Holy Spirit."[29] Here Robinson rehabilitates a perfectly Gnostic world view of continuing revelation. As another scholar neatly puts it, "Q and Thomas . . . suggest that Jesus was known initially as a teacher, a sage, a wise man, before His birth and death became part of the gospel story."[30] Simply put, this means that a primitive form of Gnostic Christianity predates the orthodox Christian gospel of Jesus as our dying and resurrected Redeemer from sin. Christian readers will be surprised to learn that they may only sing the great hymns of the faith tongue-in-cheek.

> Lord, I believe Thy precious blood,
> Which, at the mercy seat of God,
> Forever doth for sinners plead,
> For me, e'en for my soul was shed.

Such a great eighteenth-century expression of the gospel by Nicolas Zinzendorf is at best but an optional version of the meaning of Jesus; at worst, it is a secondary accretion that does not reflect our Lord's own understanding of his person and work.

This approach enables Robinson to propose in 1988, through an exegesis of what he calls Q 13:34[31] (actually Luke 13:34), a thinly veiled androgynous view of Jesus in an article entitled: "Very Goddess and Very Man: Jesus' Better Self."[32] Robinson is hopeful that this view of Jesus as the incarnation of the feminine Wisdom figure could bring "a new lease on life" for Christianity in our day.[33]

Rarely has such an enormous theological construction been based on such feeble historical grounds. Q still remains purely hypothetical.[34] The apostle Paul did not receive the Corinthian theology as a valid option. Rather he denounced it as "another gospel."[35] And the Nag Hammadi manuscripts date from the middle of the fourth century A.D. Certainly the texts were composed before this date, but the dates of composition are highly speculative and are the subject of no scholarly consensus.[36]

Confident nonetheless of the antiquity and au-

thenticity of Gnostic theology, Robinson sees the
task of modern theology as extracting values from
both trajectories (orthodox and heretical-Gnostic)
in order to produce a new formulation of Christianity for today's new situation. (One must wonder
what is new about today's situation unless it has to
do with New Age eschatology concerning the Age
of Aquarius). For Robinson this new formulation
will not look anything like the orthodox Christianity
from which he made an "exit" early on in his adult
life.[37] Thus he calls upon biblical scholars, in prepa-
ration for the twenty-first century, to "deconstruct"
their discipline, in order "to lay bare the biblicistic
presuppositions on which it was originally pro-
jected."[38] Of course with a program like this anything, including New Age "Luciferic" thinking, is
possible.[39] How beautifully this program could fit
with that of the new planetary systematic theology
of Smart and Konstantine, who describe their new-
look Christianity as "neotranscendentalist, pluralistic, social Trinitarian, universalist pantheism embedded in a soft epistemology."[40] What sounds like
a purely scholarly obligation to follow truth wher-
ever it is to be found—in Q, or in the Nag Hammadi Gnostic texts—turns out for some to be the
vehicle of a strident theological agenda. Under the
cover of scientific objectivity, the ivory tower is op-
erating a scholarly *tour de force* in the promulgation
of "another gospel."

We have not heard the last from this scholarly
"gnosticizing" view of Christian origins. A small but
growing number of very influential New Testament

scholars who apparently have never found the source of life in the classical apostolic gospel are finding in this Gnostic view of Jesus a "new lease on life." We can expect that this novel interpretation may well represent the scholarly wave of the future. If they have their way, and they probably will, under the powerful growing impact of feminism there will be a move to open the church's canon for the inclusion of a certain number of these ancient egalitarian "Christian" Gnostic documents. And then the struggle for orthodoxy will take on proportions of difficulty the church has rarely known.

A week after writing the preceding paragraph, a catalog came across my desk, announcing a new book for 1992, entitled *Five Gospels, One Jesus: What Did Jesus Really Say?*[41] Presented as a "new red letter edition" of the Gospels, the book surreptitiously "canonizes" the Gnostic *Gospel of Thomas*. Playing on ambiguity and the power of association, the publishers catalog states, "The book contains the text of the five gospels: Mark, Matthew, Luke, John and Thomas." Here, in broad daylight and living color, is the new canonical basis of New Age Christianity, proposed by the "over 100 gospel specialists" of the Jesus Seminar. The *Gospel of Thomas* now becomes a criterion for establishing the authentic teaching of Jesus. At best this will lead to canonical confusion as these two opposing versions of the gospel clash; at worst, many will seize the occasion to argue that the true Jesus was a proto-feminist, sin-denying, anti-Old Testament, anti-Creator Gnostic who came not to die for our sins but to reveal that we are all christs. The new theoretical basis is no longer theory. It is fast becoming "fact." How far away is the day when orthodox Christians will say, "That is not in the Bible," and Aquarian "Christians" will retort, "It's in ours"? Then the battle will no longer be simply *for* the Bible—it will be a battle *between* bibles.[42]

ARE WE PREPARED?

We stand again on Mars Hill,[43] surrounded by a host of unfamiliar and doubtless unfriendly gods. At some time in the future, perhaps more quickly than we think, true Christianity could well be reduced to a small minority. Christian ministry in the New Age of Aquarius will not be for the fainthearted. The defeat of ancient pagan Gnosticism and its so-called Christian counterpart was only gained by deep spirituality, hard theological work, and often physical martyrdom. But those called by Christ must stand, for they can do no other, even if it does involve similar kinds of personal sacrifice. The orthodox Christian church needs courageous leaders, not clerics of leisure and compromise. Without an extraordinary degree of prophetic commitment and self-sacrifice from a new generation of leaders, the church of Jesus Christ is no doubt headed for a period of significant persecution. If we do not speak out now, speaking out later promises to be very costly! Discerning, dedicated leaders are essential for the church in the Age of Aquarius. But not only leaders. At every level, Christians need to understand what is going on and carry that understanding to every corner of life. The world needs strong believers as never before, who will refuse to buy into the spirit of compromise that often unwittingly helps promote the New Age agenda. Unfortunately the average couch-potato Christian, so often consumed by the great American materialistic dream and nurtured by that moronic national baby sitter, TV—itself controlled by materialists and humanists serving New Age goals—would seem to be no match for the sleek, vegetarian, highly spiritual, well-read, occult-driven conspirators of the Aquarian Age.[44]

A BATTLE TO THE DEATH

The battle to the death against spiritual darkness in America defies our imagination. But, wake up, it has already begun! Tim Stafford reports the view of J. Stanley Oakes, Jr., Director of Faculty Ministries for Campus Crusade.

> [Oakes] thinks students have reason to be pessimistic. He predicts "problems like we've never seen before. Lots of Christian positions will become illegal because of multiculturalism. . . . I see a tremendous chilling effect on Christian free speech. Western civilization is being blamed for all the problems of the world. I see it as a willful, hostile, orchestrated attempt to eradicate not just Christianity from the university, but anything based on Christianity."

Oakes gives examples of the new code of student conduct adopted at 125 universities, which eliminates "hate speech," such as calling homosexuality wrong or Hinduism a false religion. Again one exception is allowed, hate speech against the Christian world view.[45] Universities wield immense power in forming the future leaders of a nation. The learned behavior of Christian students who accept the contract of silence, effectively silences Christianity on all the vital social issues of our day. Remember, as Sir Thomas More so eloquently argued in his defense against Henry VIII, silence, according to law, is consent.

I hope I am wrong, but my study of ancient Gnosticism has led me to the following conclusions. In spite of its apparently tolerant, pluralistic, and diffuse nature, the New Age has a coherent agenda, orchestrated from a diabolical center, moving and reproducing ineluctably, like algae in a lake. This ecological disaster of the spirit will lead to sudden moral and spiritual suffocation of the planet. Malcolm Muggeridge's image is graphic:

> Put frogs in some water, and . . . heat the water very slowly, so slowly that the frogs never once think of jumping out. They just quietly die once the water boils. That is what our western society is like, very gently being boiled. Therefore the impulse to jump out and save oneself is inoperative.[46]

Many unsuspecting frogs now bask in the soothing waters of New Age peace and harmony. But beware of spiritual global warming! Without

historical perspective, it is difficult to see that contemporary issues like abortion, sexual freedom, feminism, homosexuality, and multiculturalism (passed
off ingeniously as the irresistible evolution of democratic freedoms) are all related to the new one-
world Aquarian occult spirituality. All are essential
parts of a hidden, coherent agenda. Its goal is quite
simply (1) the creation of a new humanity, freed of
the inhibiting ethical, sexual, and spiritual strictures
of out-moded Christianity, and (2) by whatever
means necessary—civil law, societal pressure, false
accusation, ridicule—the elimination of faith in the
true biblical God, the Creator and Redeemer of
heaven and earth.

The rejection of God the Creator is achieved
by the eradication of all creational structures
(especially in the area of sexuality) from the
"Christianized" societies of the West in order to
bring about a repaganization of the world. Paul's
analysis in Romans 1:18-31 of the idolatry of ancient pagan society fits the present situation with
disturbing precision. If mankind at any point in
history "goes within" to worship the creature
rather than the Creator, then creation's structures
will be jettisoned and ethical and sexual perversion
will result.

The rejection of God the Redeemer is effectively achieved by denying both the reality of sin and
the historicity and redeeming significance of Christ's
cross and resurrection.

Needless to say, this diabolical program can
only end in destruction.

USING NOT BLUNTING,
THE SWORD OF THE LORD

We are certainly ill-prepared and spiritually weak. But the Lord through the apostle reminds us that "for Christ's sake [we can] delight in weaknesses, in insults, in hardships, in persecutions, in difficulties. For when [we are] weak, then [we are] strong (2 Cor. 12:10). But only those aware of and willing to take up the struggle against these spiritual forces of evil in heavenly places will be able to stand. And standing is only possible if we have the belt of truth, the breastplate of righteousness, feet shod with the gospel, the shield of faith, the helmet of salvation, and the sword of the Spirit, which is the Word of God. For us this sword will be an increasingly powerful and precious weapon for the church's survival in the Age of Aquarius.

Unfortunately many Christians today are blunting that weapon by buying into the humanistic agenda of social progress. In politics, the Southern Baptist senator Albert Gore in 1987 was a significant defender of the right to life of the unborn child. In 1986 Southern Baptist governor Bill Clinton of Arkansas wrote a letter to the local Right to Life Committee, saying, "I am opposed to abortion and to government funding for abortion."[47] These days Gore and Clinton (still Southern Baptists), have bought the whole pro-choice, pro-abortion platform of the liberal left. While Clinton's decision may well be strongly motivated by personal ambition, Gore gives evidence of deep ideological commitment. In his book, *Earth in the Balance: Ecology and the Human Spirit,* Gore's involvement in ecology is an expression of his belief in the connectedness of all things, in the great value of all religious faiths, and in his hope that ancient pagan goddess worship will help bring us planetary and personal salvation.[48] Ladies and gentlemen, please meet the first New Age contender for the presidency of the United States!

In theology, many evangelicals are adopting the view that much of what the New Testament teaches in the area of sexuality and marriage expresses the values of a society fundamentally different from our own and thus may be safely abandoned.[49] We plead with them to take another look at what is happening around us. A pagan redefinition of humanity and sexuality, explicitly opposed to the truth of God the Creator, is sweeping through the world, foreboding disastrous consequences for generations to come. In our just concerns for fair play and equality for all, is there not also the dreadful possibility that we might be participating consciously or unconsciously in the promotion of this new godless humanity? Heaven forbid!

The ancient Greco-Roman society in which Gnosticism once flourished was very much like the society in which we live today. That comparison has profound consequences for what we do with the Word of God and how we apply it to our situation. Rather than blunting this mighty Word, which spoke with such insight and redeeming power into ancient pagan culture and eventually transformed it, should we too not be using it with all our might? The New Testament writings, Paul's letters in particular, have already faced the early manifestations of Gnosticism. They gave not an inch to goddess spirituality, sexual perversions, and the destruction of creational structures in the home and in the church. Their deep understanding of the unity in God's creative and redemptive work gives us radical and potent answers, as well as a methodology, for our struggle against the same rejection of the Creator and Redeemer by New Age Gnosticism.[50] Our goal is not to preserve a romantic view of "Christian" America or to recreate a nostalgic picture of European Christendom. Nor do we want to defend any bastions of male sinfulness or insensitivity. We are to bring glory to our personal and loving God who shows his love by fashioning us according to his precise creative design, who calls us to carry the treasure of his saving presence in these earthen vessels he has made (2 Cor. 4:7), and who will one day transform them after the likeness of the glorious resurrected body of Christ (1 Cor. 15:4, 45, 53).

Paul's exhortation to the universal church, and to us, is as true now as it was then: "Finally, be strong in the Lord and in his mighty power. Put on the full armor of God so that you can take your stand against the devil's schemes" (Eph. 6:10-11). And we can do this because we know that the earth is the Lord's and the fullness thereof, and that in spite of the Devil's schemes, one day the knowledge of God (not self-*gnosis*) will fill the earth as the waters cover the sea. Then every knee, in heaven and on earth and under the earth, will bow at the mighty name of Jesus, our Savior and Lord.

NOTES

1. (Grand Rapids: Baker, 1990), 9
2. Russ Chandler, *Understanding the New Age* (Dallas: Word Publishing, 1988), 32.
3. Quoted in Tal Brooke, *When the World Will Be as One* (Eugene, Oreg.: Harvest House, 1989), 205. Gregory Donovan, in his introduction to Suresh Chander Verma's booklet, *Satanic Foundations of Hinduism and Yoga* (Kansas City, Mo.: [self-published], 1983), observes that the New Age Movement speaks of itself as an "open conspiracy" whose goals are a one-world religion and a New World Order.
4. Marilyn Ferguson, "The Quest for a New Age," review of *Heaven on Earth: Dispatches from America's Spiritual Frontier*, by Michael D'Antonio, *Los Angeles Times*, February 16, 1992, book review section, 1.
5. According to Ferguson, "An article in *American Demographics* defines New Agers as a well-educated, upscale group." She continues, "More than 90% of the subscribers to *New Age* magazine are college graduates, compared to less than half the general population. They are three times likelier than others to travel abroad and four times more likely to be active in politics or community affairs. The demographers conclude that these individuals 'are hungry for something mainstream society has not given them'" (ibid.).
6. Daniel Akst, "Freedom Is Still Rubin's Motto," *Los Angeles Times*, January 21, 1992, section D. In choosing freedom, society got more than it bargained for. As Elizabeth Achtemeier observes in noting that another of those sixties radicals, Timothy Leary, in 1989 claimed he regretted nothing: "The truth is, we have a lot to regret, and indeed, a lot of which to repent. In the 60's our society decided that drugs

were acceptable, that sex was free and that authorities were useless. 'The old taboos are dead or dying,' exulted *Newsweek* in 1967. 'The people are breaking the bonds of puritan society and helping America grow up.' We are now paying the price of that blind and irresponsible folly—in a drug war that we are not winning, in burgeoning crime that has made city neighborhoods uninhabitable, in teenage pregnancies . . . , in rampant abortions, swelling welfare rolls, sexually transmitted diseases, and countless ruined lives. We chose our own way and as with the primal choice in the garden of Eden, we brought on ourselves the way of death" ("Renewed Appreciation for an Unchanging Story," *How My Mind Has Changed*, ed. James M. Wall and David Helm [Grand Rapids: Eerdmans, 1991], 44).

7. See Tal Brooke, *Lord of the Air* (Eugene, Oreg., Harvest House, 1990), 21.

8. *Newsweek*, February 3, 1992, 86-87.

9. Ibid., 71.

10. See the books by Chandler and Brooke already cited. In the *Religious News Service*, January 4, 1992, an article, "Many Christians Found to Hold New Age Beliefs" traces a growing trend: 23 percent of Protestants and 59 percent of Roman Catholics think that New Age practices are compatible with their faith. James Davison Hunter, sociologist at the University of Virginia, in his book, *Culture Wars: The Struggle to Define America* (New York: Basic Books, 1991), states, "The institutional resources and power behind the progressive vision [which corresponds on many issues with New Age thinking] is at least as strong and probably much stronger than those favoring the orthodox." Cited in *World* 6 (February 1, 1992): 14.

11. Douglas R. Groothuis, *Unmasking the New Age* (Downers Grove, Ill.: InterVarsity, 1986), 174, says: "The new cosmic humanism of the New Age threatens to become the consensus."

12. As Tal Brooke says in his article "The Emerging Reality of a New World Order," *S.C.P. Journal* 16, 2 (1991): 15: "A 'New World Order' needs a new world government—

comprised of a world parliament, a world court, and a world police force."

13. Brooke reports the views of Ervin Laszlo, one of the founders of the Club of Rome, who in his book *Strategy for the Future: The Systems Approach to World Order* (1973) speaks of the viability of the coming world order as depending upon its "conceptual synthesis," of which there are five functions: "the mystical, the cosmological, the sociological, the pedagogical/psychological and the editorial" (Brooke, "Emerging Reality," 17 n. 77).

14. *Christian Systematic Theology* (Minneapolis: Augsburg Fortress, 1991), 440.

15. *Los Angeles Times,* February 29, 1992, A19.

16. Griscom is founder of The Light Institute in Galiskeo, New Mexico and author of *Ecstasy Is a New Frequency* (Santa Fe, N.M.: Bear and Company, 1987), in which she develops her teaching concerning the "emotional body" as well as the theory and techniques for getting in touch with one's previous lives.

17. Brooke, "Emerging Reality," 21.

18. Ibid., 17.

19. Tim Stafford, "Campus Christians and the New Thought Police," *Christianity Today,* February 10, 1992, 19.

20. Ibid., 20.

21. *Christianity Today,* February 10, 1992, 46.

22. Susan Durber, "The Female Reader of the Parables of the Lost," *Journal for the Study of the New Testament* 45 (1992): 78.

23. Rosemary Radford Ruether, *Womanguides: Readings Toward a Feminist Theology* (Boston: Beacon Press, 1985), ix.

24. Douglas R. Groothuis, *Revealing the New Age Jesus* (Downers Grove, Ill.: InterVarsity, 1990), 71.

25. James M. Robinson and Helmut Roester, *Trajectories Through Early Christianity* (Philadelphia: Fortress Press, 1971), 1-19

26. James M. Robinson, *The Nag Hammadi Library in English* (San Francisco: Harper and Row, 1977), 1.

27. See Robinson's presidential address to the Society of Biblical Literature, delivered in 1981 in San Francisco, published as "Jesus from Easter to Valentinus (or to the Apostles' Creed)," *Journal of Biblical Literature* 101 (1982): 5-37.

28. Ibid., 22.

29. Ibid., 24.

30. The opinion of Robert Funk, founder of the California-based Weststar Institute, which sponsors the Jesus Seminar, cited by Michael McAteer, *Toronto Star,* January 4, 1992, 19.

31. This is a subtle way of bestowing on hypothetical Q a seemingly objective existence (see n. 34).

32. J. M. Robinson, in *Images of the Feminine in Gnosticism,* ed. Karen L. King (Philadelphia: Fortress, 1988), 113-27.

33. Ibid., 126.

34. The noted British biblical scholar John Wenham recently stated, "No one knows for certain whether a Q-document ever existed." See his *Redating Matthew, Mark and Luke* (Downers Grove, Ill.: InterVarsity Press, 1992), 2. See also the article by S. Petrie, "Q Is Only What You Make It," *Novum Testamentum* 3 (1959), who observes tongue in cheek the myriad contradictory ways that scholars have described this unknown document: "Q is a single document; it is a composite document, incorporating earlier sources; it is used in different redactions; it is more than one document. The original language of Q is Greek; the original language of Q is Aramaic; it is used in different translations. Q is the Matthean logia; it is not the Matthean logia. Q has a definite shape; it is no more than an amorphous collection of fragments. Q is a gospel; Q is not a gospel. Q includes the crucifixion story; it does not include the crucifixion story. Q consists wholly of sayings and there is no narrative; it includes some narrative. All of Q is preserved in Matthew and Luke; not all of it is preserved; it is better preserved in Luke. Matthew's order is the correct order; Luke's order is the correct order; neither is the correct order. Q is used by Mark; it is not used by Mark"

enham, *Reading Matthew, Mark and Luke*, 42. See
icle by A. M. Farrar, "On Dispensing with Q," in
ham, ed., *Studies in the Gospels* [Oxford: University
Press, _ /5]).

35. 2 Cor. 11:4.

36. Such a major reconstruction of the picture of Jesus
is highly speculative. Thomas is dated at the very earliest in
the middle of the second century. Many scholars put it later,
while Koester pushes it into the first century, though without
any evidence (see both E. Yamauchi, *Pre-Christian Gnosticism*
[Grand Rapids: Eerdmans, 1973], 35, and H. Koester, "The
Gospel of Thomas," *The Nag Hammadi Library* [New York:
Harper and Row, 1977], 117). And Q, even in the above-men-
tioned article, is described by Funk as "a hypothetical gospel."
Q is indeed hypothetical, and on two levels. It is an enormous
jump of logic to describe Q as a gospel, with the idea that it
circulated independently and functioned like the Gospels we
know. Q has no beginning or end, no literary artifice. At best
it is a handy collection of some of Jesus' sayings. On a second
level Q is hypothetical because no one has ever seen it. It is
merely an academic construct that some scholars even consider unnecessary because unfounded (see n. 34). But such an
extraordinarily weak base is seriously presented for justifying
a radically different picture of Jesus than that of the canonical
Gospels. There is clearly another agenda than merely that of
historical evidence, what Funk piously calls "a forthright ex-
ploration of the real figure of Jesus behind many of the images of Him created after, and in some cases, in spite of the
facts." Behind all the scientific posturing, there is another dog-
matic image of Jesus being championed, namely, the Gnostic
New Age Jesus. Thus the association of Q with the *Gospel of
Thomas* is high-order speculation. One must speculate that Q
existed; one must also speculate about its theological orienta-
tion—that Jesus was only a wisdom teacher (though some
scholars maintain that Q includes part of the account of the
death of Jesus; also, even if one granted the existence of Q,
these sayings of Jesus were used in orthodox circles, and thus

they did not circulate alone); furthermore, one must speculate on a hypothetical relationship between Q and the *Gospel of Thomas*. The result of all this speculation is placed on the same footing as the apostolic gospel (which in its formulation in 1 Cor. 15:3-5 dates from the forties or thirties in Palestine) as an alternate or even more original understanding of Jesus.

37. J. M. Robinson, "How My Mind Has Changed," *SBL 1985 Seminar Papers*, ed. Kent Harold Richards (Atlanta, Ga.: Scholars Press, 1985), 486.

38. Ibid., 495.

39. Helmut Koester, who has spearheaded with Robinson this relativizing "trajectories" approach to early Christianity (see their *Trajectories Through Early Christianity* [Minneapolis: Fortress Press, 1971]), in the epilogue of the collection of essays in his honor, *The Future of Early Christianity* (Minneapolis: Fortress Press, 1991), gives his own prospective for future directions in the New Testament field. Building on his view of early Christianity as "just one of several Hellenistic propaganda religions, competing with others who seriously believed in their god and who also imposed moral standards on their followers" (473), he calls upon New Testament scholars no longer to consider the New Testament canon "as part of a special book that is different from other early Christian writings," in order to allow the other early Christian voices—"heretics, Marcionites, Gnosticism, Jewish Christians, perhaps also women. . . . to be heard again" (472). Koester readily and openly admits that New Testament interpretation is not value-free, objective science. The historical-critical method was "designed as a hermeneutical tool for the liberation from conservative prejudice and from the power of ecclesiastical and political institutions" (474). In the same way, future New Testament studies should have as their goal "political and religious renewal . . . inspired by the search for equality, freedom and justice" in the "comprehensive political perspective" of our modern world (475-76).

40. Ibid., 441.

41. Robert W. Funk and Roy W. Hoover, *Five Gospels, One Jesus: What Did Jesus Really Say?* (Sonoma, Calif.: Polebridge Press, 1992).

42. It will be surprising if, in the near future, we do not see biblical commentary series including commentaries on *Thomas* and perhaps other Gnostic texts. Already *Hermeneia: A Critical and Historical Commentry on the Bible,* ed. Helmut Koester (Philadelphia: Fortress) includes a volume entitled *Ignatius of Antioch: A Commentary on the Seven Letters of Ignatius* by William R. Schoedel (1985). Schoedel admits that the series "identifies itself as a 'critical and historical commentary on the Bible,'" and grants that the letters of Ignatius have never been among the biblical books. They are, however, "close to the canonical writings. . . . but canonical lines do not correspond in any very precise way to historical demarcations, and there can be no escape from including the widest possible range of relevant material in our investigation of the emergence of the church in the Graeco-Roman world" (xi). No doubt there will be "no escape from including" a volume or two on the Nag Hammadi texts.

43. Norman Geisler's provocative image, in David K. Clark and Norman L. Geisler, *Apologetics in the New Age: A Christian Critique of Pantheism* (Grand Rapids: Baker, 1990), 7.

44. In spite of the vast number of Christian believers, one gets the impression that they are out-maneuvered on every side by humanist civil rights groups. A recent poll showed 78 percent of Americans favoring voluntary Bible classes on school grounds and voluntary Christian fellowship groups, while 73 percent want prayer before athletic games (*Christianity Today,* February 10, 1992, 55). And yet all the major gains in social legislation concerning religion and the creational structures on which the Christian faith is built seem to go in the other direction.

45. Stafford, "Campus Christians," 20; see also Oakes's short article in *Table Talk,* March 1992, 12.

46. Malcolm Muggeridge, "Dialogues with Malcolm Muggeridge," *S.C.P. Journal* 16, 2 (1991): 37.

47. Evangelical Press Service, cited in *Southern Californian Christian Times* (August 1992), 8.

48. Al Gore, *Earth in the Balance: Ecology and the Human Spirit* (New York: Houghton Mifflin, 1992), 258-60. In his chapter "Environmentalism of the Spirit" Gore also quotes favorably Pierre Teilhard de Chardin, the excommunicated Jesuit theologian, who is often cited by New Age authors. Gore attempts to mix Southern Baptist theology with New Age spirituality. While affirming that God is the Creator, Gore manages, in typical pantheistic fashion, to confuse the Creator with the creation. Using the example of the hologram, so dear to New Age philosophy, Gore proposes to show how God is manifest in the world. "Each tiny portion of the hologram contains a tiny representation of the entire three-dimensional image. However . . . when one looks . . . at the entire hologram, these thousands of tiny faint images come together in the eye of the beholder as a single large vivid image." God is thus the sum total of all created things.

Gore is certainly moving in the "right" circles. He was in Rio at the Earth Summit and in his address said, "The environmental crisis is fundamentally a spiritual crisis" (see Tom Heyden, "Spirituality Infuses Hope for the Earth," *Los Angeles Times,* June 18, 1992). He is pictured in the *New Age Journal* ([July/August 1992], 70) with leaders of the "Joint Appeal by Religion and Science," a movement headquartered at the Cathedral of St. John the Divine in New York City, a liberal Episcopal church often associated with New Age causes. According to Constance Cumbey (*The Hidden Dangers of the Rainbow* [Lafayette, La.: Huntington House, 1983], 139), David Spangler, the New Age Satanist, preached there (see also 24).

49. See, for instance, the change in direction taken by the evangelical scholar, A. Lincoln, professor of New Testament at Sheffield University, England. In his book *Paradise Now and Not Yet* (Society for New Testament Studies Monograph Series 43 [Cambridge: University Press, 1981]), Lincoln found little problem with the Pauline authorship of

Ephesians (if one allows some freedom to a secretary, and the fact of a liturgical and baptismal setting). Also, Paul's teaching on marriage was massively affirmed: "It can readily be seen that the standard and prototype for such instructions [concerning the relationship between husbands and wives] is [not the Greco-Roman form but] the marriage between the heavenly bridegroom and the Church, and that Paul 'is arguing from the Heavenly Marriage to the human marriage, not vice-versa: he is seeing the human in the light of the heavenly, and therefore will have the human model itself on the heavenly'" (163, quoting C. Chavasse, *The Bride of Christ* [London, 1940], 77).

In his recent (1990) commentary on Paul's Epistle to the Ephesians, Lincoln now maintains that Paul is not the author of Ephesians. The authentic Paul's teaching on marriage takes another, essentially contradictory approach than that of the unknown author of Ephesians. For instance, while the authentic Paul favored women in leadership, Ephesians does not (391). Lincoln concludes, "It is best, then, to see this vision of marriage [in Ephesians] for what it is—conditioned by the cultural assumptions of its time [the Greco-Roman world—see 390] . . . bringing its interpretation of the Pauline gospel to bear on the household structures of its society to produce a distinctive adaptation of those structures. Contemporary Christians can best appropriate it by realizing that they are to attempt to do something similar in their own setting—to bring to bear what they hold to be the heart of the Christian message on the marriage conventions of their time [i.e., "the egalitarian and feminist climate of contemporary society"—392]. . . . By candidly acknowledging one's own contemporary Christian perspective, one is free not to allow the writer's analogy with Christ and the Church . . . to straitjacket subsequent reflection on the passage, but instead to decide which elements of his vision might remain of value and which are now outmoded. An appropriation of this text . . . might well reject the hierarchical elements in the exhortations about roles and the corresponding application of hierarchical elements of the relationship between Christ and the Church" (*Word Biblical Commentary 42, Ephesians* [Waco, Tex.: Word Books, 1990], 392-93).

What can explain these major changes in the space of nine years. As far as authorship is concerned, no new documents have been discovered proving that Paul is *not* the author of Ephesians. Defending the Pauline authorship of Colossians and Ephesians has been one of the mainstays of evangelical New Testament science (see Donald Guthrie, *New Testament Introduction* [Downers Grove, Ill: InterVarsity Press, 1973], 479-521, 545-63, and 584-634, and more recently D. A. Carson, D. J. Moo and L. Morris, *An Introduction to the New Testament* [Grand Rapids: Zondervan, 1992]). Yet more and more evangelicals of the feminist persuasion are denying Pauline authorship of these letters which make clear statements concerning differentiated gender roles in the church. For the Pastorals, see R. C. Kroeger and C. C. Kroeger, *I Suffer Not a Woman* (Grand Rapids: Baker, 1992), 46 and elsewhere, where the authors are not a little vague on this question. Lincoln's decision concerning the authorship of Ephesians is not pure science. It too has theological fallout. Just as the author of Ephesians "adapted" Paul's gospel to his time, so we may adapt Paul to our time.

A far as Lincoln's rejection of Ephesians's teaching on sexual roles and marriage is concerned, the reason is honestly and openly admitted—"the egalitarian and feminist climate of contemporary society." But one has to wonder why Lincoln gives such a major role to contemporary society in determining what is husk and what is kernel in the Bible, especially in light of the godless direction contemporary society is taking.

50. This indeed is one of the major weaknesses in Kroeger and Kroeger, *I Suffer Not.* Having described the heresy facing "Paul" in the Pastorals, they dismiss his teaching for our day, since he was supposedly dealing with an extreme heresy that does not concern us. They fail to see that the heresy they describe has returned in an even more extreme

form of New Age "Christian" feminism, and that it is posing as much of a threat today as it did in the time of Paul. Needless to say, Paul's ancient answer finds a surprisingly relevant application in our own time.